THE IMPERIAL RESIDENCES
around Saint Petersburg

THE IMPERIAL
RESIDENCES
around Saint Petersburg

FOREWORD BY MIKHAIL PIOTROVSKY

ESSAYS BY NINA VERNOVA (Peterhof),
LARISA BARDOVSKAYA (Tsarskoye Selo),
NIKOLAI TRETYAKOV (Pavlovsk),
YURY MUDROV (Oranienbaum),
VLADIMIR SEMIONOV (Gatchina)

TRANSLATED FROM THE RUSSIAN BY
PAUL WILLIAMS (foreword and essays)
and VALERY FATEYEV (captions)

DESIGN AND LAYOUT BY VASILY BERTELS

PHOTOGRAPHS BY
LEONID BOGDANOV, SERGEI CHABUTKIN, VLADIMIR DAVYDOV,
PAVEL DEMIDOV, VLADIMIR DENISOV, VLADIMIR DOROKHOV,
VLADIMIR GORDT, ALEXANDER GRONSKY, PAVEL IVANOV,
ALEXANDER KASHNITSKY, ROMUALD KIRILLOV, VLADIMIR
MELNIKOV, ALEXANDER MININ, YURY MOLODKOVETS,
VILLY ONIKUL, NIKOLAI RAKHMANOV, VICTOR SAVIK,
GRIGORY SHABLOVSKY, GEORGY SHLAKAN,
YEVGENY SINIAVER, AND OLEG TRUBSKY

EDITED BY MARIA LYZHENKOVA
COMPUTER LAYOUT BY IRINA SEROVA
COLOUR CORRECTION BY VITALY VYAZOVSKY,
TATYANA KRAKOVSKAYA and PETER KRAKOVSKY

MANAGING EDITOR: NINA GRISHINA

Alfa-Colour Art Publishers thanks the Peterhof, Tsarskoye Selo,
Pavlovsk, Oranienbaum and Gatchina Museum Complexes
for lending transparencies.

Films produced by Goland Company, St Petersburg

PRINTED AND BOUND IN FINLAND

ISBN 5-94795-007-3

THE IMPERIAL RESIDENCES
around Saint Petersburg

· PETERHOF · TSARSKOYE SELO·
· PAVLOVSK · ORANIENBAUM · GATCHINA·

· ALFA-COLOUR ART PUBLISHERS ·
· SAINT PETERSBURG 2003 ·

The

suburbs of St Petersburg are famous for their palace and park ensembles. The five imperial residences — Peterhof, Tsarskoye Selo, Pavlovsk, Oranienbaum and Gatchina — are each unique and magnificent in their own way. Their remarkable palaces and astonishing parks cannot fail to affect anyone who seeks to picture Russian history and feel the spirit of the era in which a particular residence was created. Each of the names creates a particular image in the minds of Petersburgers and all those who appreciate Russian history and culture.

Peterhof is all Peter the Great, his striving for the vast expanses of the sea and the rather unsophisticated luxury that symbolizes the attainment of the secrets of European civilization and the victorious might of a state seeking its place on the world stage. The history of Russia is in its palaces, the fates, brilliant and bitter, of the nation's rulers. Oranienbaum embodies the image of Peter's time and preserves the memory of the strange era of his successors. Tsarskoye Selo is the brilliant face of Catherine II's great state, the noble tread of Alexander I's time and the tragic fate of the last emperor, Nicholas II. The spirit of Pushkin abides here, as do the strange visions of Anna Akhmatova. Pavlovsk embodied in its palaces, monuments and impressive landscapes the refined spirit of Paul I that his contemporaries failed to understand and the brilliant talents and minds of the finest architects and gardeners. Gatchina is full of the fantastic elegance of Antonio Rinaldi, the chivalry of Paul and the tragic self-isolation of Alexander III.

Around the new capital of the Russian Empire, these palaces and parks became inseparably bound in a wreath without which the capital could not then have existed and cannot now be imagined. Works of art migrated from one palace to another and all of them together were St Petersburg — beautiful, fantastic and, at the same time, tragic.

The palace-and-park ensembles were struck a terrible blow by the enemy forces in the middle of the twentieth century and in sacrificing themselves saved the city and its treasures. Their resurrection from the ruins has been no less fantastic an event than the creation of St Petersburg which embraces the Winter Palace and the Hermitage, Peterhof and Monplaisir, Tsarskoye Selo and the Lyceum, Oranienbaum and the Coasting Hill, Pavlovsk and the Temple of Friendship and Gatchina and the Priory Palace. The spirit of the city is reborn in them time and again, bringing inspiration and faith. The tireless labour of the museum staff, gardeners and restorers is one of the noblest occupations on Earth as it gives people knowledge and aesthetic pleasure.

The suburbs of St Petersburg with their palace-and-park ensembles are an image of our past and future, our common concern and our shared joy.

Mikhail Piotrovsky

PETERHOF

T he column by the railing of the Upper Park at Peterhof bears two figures: *26* and *29*. The first indicates versts, the second kilometres. That is the distance from the Obvodny Canal, the old boundary of St Petersburg, to the splendid suburban residence of the Russian emperors that is today a museum, the world-famous palace-and-park ensemble that is a monument of Russian national culture of the eighteenth and nineteenth centuries.

Peterhof stands on the southern shore of the Gulf of Finland. The parks created here over two centuries cover an area of some 1,000 hectares. Two of them, the oldest Lower Park and nineteenth-century Alexandria extend along the shoreline. The sea here dropped in stages to its present level, leaving a series of terraces. This feature of the landscape made it possible to lay out parks on two levels.

Since its foundation by Peter the Great, this official summer residence of the Russian rulers came to be graced by more than ten palace buildings, elegant park pavilions, and a unique hydraulic system that allowed the installation of more than 150 fountains. The result was a complex that accorded with Peter's goal of creating a residence no less luxurious than that of the French kings at Versailles. The fountains built early in the eighteenth century have been functioning for almost three hundred years and are still famous despite the appearance of elaborate systems elsewhere in the world.

Peterhof is only two years younger than Russia's northern capital. In May 1703, Peter founded the city in the lands at the mouth of the Neva newly recovered from Sweden. To guard against attack from the sea, that same year work began on the construction of a naval fortress, the forerunner of Kronstadt, on Kotlin Island. Peter often visited the construction site, shortening the crossing in bad weather by travelling along the southern shore.

Here there was a manor that came to be known as Peterhof – "Peter's Court". The first mention of it in the Tsar's *Campaign Journal* is dated 13 September 1705. The idea of creating a suburban residence here came later. Construction of the Upper Chambers (the future Great Palace) and Monplaisir began only in 1714.

The role of the Great Palace as the architectural centre of a vast ensemble was not determined at the outset. In 1714, when the building of the Sea Canal and construction of the Grotto and Cascade had begun, work started on the Hilltop or Upper Chambers. The original design was by Johann Braunstein drawing on the concept put forward by the French architect Alexandre Le Blond. The palace was relatively small and in 1721 Niccolo Michetti, Le Blond's successor as chief architect, presented plans for its reconstruction. Still, that provided only a temporary solution to the problem of accommodating the growing court.

In 1745 Empress Elizabeth ordered another reconstruction of the Upper Chambers, entrusting the work to her favourite architect, Bartolomeo Francesco Rastrelli. He removed the wooden structures and the masonry pavilions and galleries, leaving only the central part of Peter's palace untouched.

Work on the new palace began in 1745, and by 1755 all the finishing was complete. Grand festivities were held here in 1756. The palace rises on the edge of a 16-metre-high terrace. It has a superb pedestal in the form of the glittering statuary and sparkling water of the Great Cascade. The size and opulence of the rooms created by the brilliant architect and hundreds of first-rate craftsmen produced a stunning impression. The layout of the gala residence fully accorded with the idea of court life as a never-ending theatrical performance.

The gilded main staircase led to a no less opulent Ballroom, then to the new Vestibule, again decorated with gilded carving and ceiling paintings. Turning right, guests found themselves on the axis of the enfilade of state rooms. This seemed endless, especially as the last room had a large window, allowing the eye to travel on unhindered into the park.

Rastrelli's creations appeared in the final decade when the Baroque style dominated and consequently many were doomed to a brief existence. The new Classical style with its very differ-

South of the Great Palace lies the Upper Garden, extending over 15 hectares, as far as the highway to St Petersburg where its main entrance is marked by splendid pylons. The green lawns and fountain basins arranged about the axis of the garden in the broad central parterre form a splendid ensemble with the palace, the garden performing the function of a grand courtyard – a *cour d'honneur*.

In Peter's time, as at other suburban residences, the garden was used for growing vegetables, culinary and even medicinal herbs. The three large ponds that have come down to us somewhat changed were used not only as reservoirs in the fountain system, but also for keeping live fish. In its early days, then, the Upper Garden had primarily practical functions.

It acquired a different character later in the century. The vegetable plots disappeared, giving way to the trimmed trees and shrubs, pergolas (covered alleys) and arbours of a true formal garden. The most important element, though, in the transformation of a kitchen garden into something much grander was the installation of richly decorated fountains. For a quarter century from 1734, when Paul Sualem suggested putting a round basin between the existing square ponds, work never ceased in the Upper Garden. The next year Carlo Bartolomeo Rastrelli (the architect's father) created the Oak Fountain, and two years later sculptural groups adorned the square ponds. A further fountain with a round basin was placed further south on the axis of the garden, this time with a sculptural group in the centre. Thus, the composition of five fountains was formed that, with a succession of changes in decoration, has come down to us today. An important feature of the Upper Garden was added in 1755–59 by Rastrelli junior – the tall railing that encloses it on three sides.

In the middle of the Upper Garden is a large rectangular basin, with semicircular projections on its short sides. In 1799 the remarkable sculptural group *Neptune* was set up in its centre. This work had been acquired by the future Paul I in 1782 in Nuremberg, where it was created in the seventeenth century by Christoph Ritter and Georg Schweigger. The god of the sea stands on a high pedestal, the trident in his right hand pointed downwards. At his feet are nymphs, symbolizing the rivers Pegnitz and Rednitz that join near Nuremberg, sitting on barrels, two figures riding hippocampi and four putti on dolphins and sea-dragons.

Following the ravages of the Second World War, the Upper Garden was recreated using the axonometric plans drawn in 1775 by the noted mathematician and cartographer Pierre de Saint-Hilaire for Catherine the Great.

The first general blueprint for Peterhof was compiled by Braunstein in 1716. Surviving drawings by Peter the Great, his orders and comments on documents, strongly suggest that Peter

ent set of ideals that spread rapidly across Russia in the 1760s prompted the reconstruction of interiors in the Great Palace. In 1766–77 Jean-Baptiste Vallin de La Mothe decorated two Chinese Cabinets here, adjoining the Hall of Peter's time in the centre of the palace. Particularly large alterations were made in the 1770s by Yury Velten. He substantially changed the décor in a number of living apartments and state rooms: the Throne Hall, Dining-Room and Vestibule. This was no easy task as the architect was expected to decorate in Classical style without changing the proportions of the rooms, the number and shape of the windows, or the pattern of the parquet floors. He passed the test with flying colours. For the next 65 years no major changes were made to the halls of the Great Palace. Only in 1845, in anticipation of his daughter Olga's wedding, did Nicholas I decide to have some things refurbished and reworked. The plans, drawn up by Andrei Stakenschneider, were implemented by 1850.

Two centuries of work on the imperial residence produced a palace in which there co-existed interiors that had for the most part retained the look of Peter's time, glittering halls from the mid-eighteenth century, calm, austere halls of the Classical period and others from the mid-nineteenth century that revived the principles of the Rococo. As this combination was produced by outstanding architects, the palace does not produce an impression of jarring eclecticism, but in some astonishing manner comes together to form a complex and attractive whole.

In the eighteenth and nineteenth centuries, the Great Palace at Peterhof was the central edifice of the official "crown" residence of the Russian rulers. Its halls were the setting for many important events, festivities and receptions, balls and masquerades that amazed guests with their opulent luxury.

himself was responsible for the general layout of the park, and sometimes the detailed planning of certain features of the Upper Chambers and Monplaisir.

In 1720 work began on the Marly Palace that not only determined the western limit of the park, but also provided an architectural centre from which three alleys would later radiate across the Lower Park. A year later the foundations of the first Russian Hermitage were laid close to the sea. The finely proportioned two-storey building stands within a deep moat crossed only by a light bridge. The Hermitage, its French name suggesting "a place of solitude", was intended for entertaining the Tsar's closest confidants. The idea came from Peter's travels in Europe where such buildings were in fashion. Braunstein only completed the Hermitage in the summer of 1725, after Peter's death, and on 26 July his widow, Catherine I, visited the pavilion. Everything here was devised by her husband: the lift mechanisms, the two oak balconies and the table for 14 diners.

The terrace to the north of the Great Palace provides a unparalleled view across the Lower Park to the sea. In the centre is the glistening Great Cascade. Left and right lie the Great Flower Gardens with their bowl fountains. Rising in front of the cascade is the mighty jet of the Samson Fountain, while beyond it the canal runs arrow-straight to the sea. The canal divides the 102-hectare park into two roughly equal parts. Following Peter's concept, after 1714 Braunstein and Michetti created an elaborate network of alleys, flower beds, a drainage system, basins and fountains on the marshy shore of the Gulf of Finland. Between 1715 and 1738 all the gardening work was directed by the master-gardener Leonard Garnichfelt who had been invited from Holland. He trained a team of Russian gardeners who created a masterpiece of a regular Baroque park here. The eastern part of the Lower Park contains the Monplaisir Palace, the Catherine Block, the Chessboard Hill Cascade and Roman Fountains, the Pyramid, Sun and trick fountains. The western part contains the Hermitage and Marly Palace, the Golden Hill and Lion Cascades, the Ménager and Cloche Fountains. Alleys running off at angles to the Hermitage and Monplaisir formed, together with the Sea Canal, another "trident" linking the terrace and the shore.

The main north-south axis of the Lower Park is the Sea Canal. It begins in a harbour placed a considerable distance out into the gulf and, running between dikes for part of its length, crosses the park to the foot of the Great Cascade. Faced with granite and adorned by gilded masks and fountains, it is one of the main sites of Peterhof, graphically demonstrating the geographic and

aesthetic link between the maritime residence and watery element. The canal, completed in the main by 1721, became a transport artery and a formal entrance to the park. With the installation of the Samson Fountain in the basin at the foot of the Great Cascade in 1735, using the canal to reach the Great Palace became problematic.

The Great Cascade is the centre of the tremendous system of fountains at Peterhof. Its size, the volume of water, the richness of the sculptural decoration, striking variety of jets and, finally, the striking, eloquent harmony of all its parts makes it outstanding among the world's historical fountain installations. It is a superb work of Baroque art whose sculptures vividly express the main idea of the Peterhof ensemble – glorification of Russia's victories in the struggle to gain access to the Baltic.

The idea of an arrangement of cascades and grottoes was conceived by Peter the Great. It was proposed to construct two grottoes and two stepped cascades, delivering their waters into the basin linked by the canal to the sea. Construction of the Lower Grotto began in May 1716, the year after the canal. When Le Blond arrived in Peterhof, he suggested adding jets to the steps of the cascade to increase the volume of water and adding fountains in front of the Lower Grotto.

Work on the grotto was completed in June 1720. Following Michetti's plans it was embellished with stones and seashells, and the balustrade with vases. Slightly later two masks with bowls appeared on the terrace above the Lower Grotto and the Upper Grotto was created there too. Michetti reduced the number of steps in the cascade to seven, and suggested adorning the walls below them with bas-reliefs. In 1723 a 17-jet fountain was installed in front of the entrance to the Lower Grotto.

The cascade was tested in Peter's presence on 13 July 1721, and began functioning regularly in August 1723, although work was still going on. After Peter's death, his ideas continued to be realized. In 1738, for example, a group of two tritons blowing conches by Rastrelli senior was installed above the Lower Grotto. The decision to create the Samson Fountain was taken back in 1734, the twenty-fifth anniversary of the Battle of Poltava. That key victory in the Northern War took place on 27 June 1709, the Orthodox feast day of St Sampsonius, which prompted the idea of depicting the event allegorically through the Old Testament hero Samson's victory over the lion. Rastrelli completed the central figure only in 1735, however.

With time, the sculptures became dilapidated and the fountains in the grotto stopped working. It was only at the end of the eighteenth century that Paul I turned his attention to Peterhof. On 19 August 1799 he gave instructions for the replacement of the lead sculpture with bronze. The work, in which the leading Russian sculptors of the day participated, was completed by July 1806.

Fourteen statues were cast from plaster copies of ancient originals kept in the Academy of Arts. The group *Bacchus and a Satyr* reproduced Michelangelo's celebrated work. Nine statues and one group were cast from original models by Feodosy Shchedrin, Jacques Dominique Rachette, Fedot Shubin, Ivan Prokofiev and Ivan Martos. The old lead sculpture was left in some places – the bas-reliefs on the steps, the frogs and Rastrelli's masks. While the sculptors were prominent members of the Classical academic school, the treatment of many figures, full of lively movement, suited them splendidly for inclusion in the Baroque creation.

In the eastern park of the Lower Park a high artificial terrace, reinforced by immense granite boulders, protrudes into the sea, surmounted by a single-storey brick building with a tall roof. Two narrower galleries with pavilions at the end run from the central block. The walls of the galleries are pierced by narrow French windows, alternating with deep semicircular niches emphasizing the solidity of walls built to withstand the north wind. On the land side the galleries are in line with the central section and form a sort of airy arcade. Here on the south there is a snug little garden with flower beds and fountains – the Wheatsheaf in the centre surrounded by four identical ones . It is bordered on the east by the Guest Gallery, the Bathhouse Block and Assembly Hall with service premises; on the west by another gallery of the same kind and the palatial building known as the Catherine Wing.

This complex, dating mainly from the mid-eighteenth century, is known as Monplaisir, from the French meaning "my pleasure". Properly the name belongs to the small amusement palace on the terrace that is as old as Peterhof itself. Its foundation marked the start of the whole ensemble. The palace was a favourite place of Peter the Great and he gave it its name. Peter chose the site and drew up the plan. It would be hard to find anywhere else that has so fully retained the imprint of the tastes, habits and pursuits of the Reformer-Tsar.

As with a number of other buildings of the period, there is no clear information on who designed Monplaisir. Peter's drawings are no more than expressions of his wishes, while many researchers point to the celebrated Andreas Schlüter, who worked in Russia about a year before his death in 1714, as the architect. In any event, the construction and finishing was supervised by his assistant Johann Braunstein. The palace was completed by August 1723, when the first major festivities were held at Peterhof. In contrast to the plain façades, the interior was richly and variously decorated. Fine ceiling paintings, delicate stucco work, the unexpectedly brilliant Chinese Cabinet, the tiled walls and elaborate parquet floors all impressed Peter's guests. The impression was enhanced by the collections of European painting, Oriental porcelain and furniture that the Emperor had had sent from Europe.

First of all there was a vegetable plot to the west of the Monplaisir flower garden, then it was replaced by a brick-built greenhouse. In 1748 Rastrelli used the foundations of the greenhouse to construct a palatial building larger and more spacious than Monplaisir for Empress Elizabeth to hold balls and receptions in. In the 1780s Quarenghi redecorated the main rooms there, while in the early nineteenth century Domenico Scotti painted some of the ceilings and covings in grisaille technique. In the adjoining wooden galleries the personal apartments of Catherine II have survived. She lived here before 27 June 1762 when she hurried to St Petersburg to raise the Guards and depose her husband, Peter III. In memory of her time here, the building has become known as the Catherine Block. In her reign it was used for banquets and the annual ball for graduates of the Smolny Institute.

One more palace from Peter's time, the Marly, stands in the western part of the Lower Park. Despite its small size, it plays a great role as the focal point of three alleys crossing the park. The palace is the centre of its own small ensemble, including two gardens, a cascade and fountains on a parterre in front of it.

Work began here with the construction of two ponds, one rectangular, one semicircular. The excavated earth went into a huge embankment along the shore of the gulf that provided protection against the sea and the north wind. The semicircular pond was divided internally into four sectors. This work was completed by 1722. Apart from their aesthetic function, the ponds also served a practical purpose, being used to keep pike-perch and various kinds of carp.

In 1720 Braunstein produced plans for a palace to stand on the strip of land between the rectangular Marly Pond and the Sectoral Ponds and by 1723 the one-storey building raised on a basement was in the main complete. The new palace was called Marly after the French royal residence of Marly-le-Roi outside Paris. From the mid-eighteenth century, the palace, built to accommodate exalted guests, turned into a sort of museum or repository containing Peter the Great's wardrobe, gifts presented to him and everyday items associated with the founder of Peterhof.

Each of the four palaces in the Lower Park was supposed to have a corresponding cascade. While the Marly was being built, Peter gave detailed instructions on this score. Michetti followed these scrupulously and designed a cascade with a statue of Hercules overcoming the seven-headed Hydra at the top. Carlo Bartolomeo Rastrelli cast three Medusa masks and cartouches for it. Then the pace of work slowed, stopping altogether in 1727. In 1731–32 the architect Mikhail Zemtsov completed construction of the cascade. White marble steps with gold risers, descending 14 metres, sculpture and stone steps with balustrades make an exceptionally striking combination. Besides the masks, five marble and two gilded statues adorn the cascade. These include notable works by Pietro Baratta (*Andromeda* and *Flora*) and Antonio Tarsia (*Neptune*, *Triton* and *Nymph*). Zemtsov installed gilded copper sheets beneath the steps, creating an interesting play of light through the falling water. The cascade became known as the Golden Hill. In the parterre at its foot huge columns of water rise from the centre of large round basins, while glittering in the spray around are four gilded tritons that give the fountains their name.

Symmetrically placed at the junctions of main alleys in the Lower Park are two identically decorated fountains – *Adam* and *Eve*. The sculptures are free copies of the famous works by Antonio Rizzi that still adorn the Palace of the Doges in Venice, produced to order by the Italian Giovanni Bonazza in 1717.

At the end of the alley leading south from Monplaisir, the Chessboard Hill Cascade descends the terrace. Above and below it are entrances to grottoes, the top one guarded by the dragons. Powerful jets of water spurt from their mouths and run down the steps. The edges of the cascade and upper grotto are lined with tufa, while to the right of the wooden steps ten marble statues of ancient gods stand. Work on the cascade began soon after Peterhof was founded, but proceeded slowly. It was only completed in 1739 to Zemtsov's design and called the Dragon Hill. Soon after, however, the steps were painted in a chequerboard pattern and it acquired its present name. In 1875 the dragons were remade in metal from drawings by Nikolai Benois.

The area below the cascade is adorned by some of the most attractive fountains in Peterhof. Constructed in 1738–39, to the design of the architects Blank and Davydov, they greatly resemble the fountains on St Peter's Square in Rome and hence became known as the Roman Fountains. In 1756 Rastrelli redesigned the fountains while retaining the basic idea. Their decoration includes various types of coloured marble and sculptural elements – gilded lead garlands, wreaths and masks cast in 1817 from models by Ivan Martos.

The Hermitage quickly acquired its cascade, created by Michetti in 1720. It was called the Lion Cascade on account of its sculptural decoration. It only began functioning in 1799–1800, however, when the architect Andrei Voronikhin relocated it. He added eight vases to the low stone wall and statues of Hercules and Flora that were replaced two years later by guardian lions. In the 1850s Stakenschneider redesigned the cascade introducing tall Ionic columns of grey granite with Carrara marble bases and capitals and, between them, twelve fountains with marble bowls.

Despite the problems caused by the harsh climate and flooding, by 1723 the Lower Park greatly impressed the visitors to Peterhof. The French ambassador, Campredon, wrote to Louis XV of the astonishing speed with which the residence was being created. He added the words Peter said to him on the balcony of the Upper Chambers: "At your Versailles you do not have such a marvellous view as here, where on the one side there is the sea with Kronstadt, and on the other St Petersburg is seen."

Peter entrusted the creation of a water supply to Vasily Tuvolkov who had studied hydraulics in Holland and France. A survey of the area revealed several bodies of water about twenty kilometres to the south, near the villages of Kipen and Ropsha, that were fed by springs. Over the summer of 1721 sluices and a canal were built that, on 9 August that year, brought water to Peterhof. Since the land gradually drops northwards from Ropsha, the water naturally flows to the reservoirs in the Upper Garden, where only low fountains can be created. The Lower

Yegor Botman
Portrait of Nicholas I. 1849. Oil on canvas

Peterhof. Alexandria
The Gothic Chapel (Church of St Alexander
Nevsky). Architects: Karl Friedrich Schinkel,
Adam Menelaws, Joseph Charlemagne, 1830–34

Park is 16 metres further down and, by the principle of communicating vessels, the water piped from the basins surges powerfully upwards, providing the host of tall jets below the terrace. The principle and method of supplying water discovered by Peter are still operating today as evidence of the talent of Peterhof's founder. Construction of the fountains and improvement of the system went on until the mid-nineteenth century. In the end the Lower Park had 147 fountains and four cascades, the Upper Garden five fountains and one cascade.

A special feature of Peterhof is the eighteenth-century trick fountains. Nowhere else in the world has such a number survived, although in their time they were an almost obligatory feature of a regular park. The first such practical joke was the Little Oak (1802) surrounded by five tulips and two benches. Someone strolling in the park would be attracted by the bright flowers, bending to examine them he would be squirted with water. Stepping back towards the tree, he would find its leaves and branches suddenly spurting water too. When he sought the safety of the benches, two jets rose from them and arced over him. Nearby are three other artificial trees – firs from 1784 that constantly produce silvery streams. Nearby is the Umbrella Fountain dating from 1796.

The Pyramid Fountain is particularly striking for its volume and shape. Set in the depths of the eastern part of the Lower Park, from a distance it resembles some triumphal monument. It was created by Michetti in 1724, inspired by a three-sided version Peter had seen at Versailles.

East of the Lower Park on the shore of the gulf lies the 115-hectare Alexandria Park. In contrast to the grand, official, noisy show of its neighbour, here everything is calm and quiet. Alexandria was conceived and created in the second quarter of the nineteenth century as a rural retreat, the private estate of the Romanovs. In August 1825 Alexander I gave the land here to his brother Nicholas, who, when he became emperor soon after, presented them to his wife Alexandra Fiodorovna. The park takes its name from her. In 1826 the Tsar and his family decided to build a "little country house" here. The work was entrusted to Adam Menelaws, an architect of Scottish origin, and the master-gardeners Wendelsdorf, Gombel and Erler. In keeping with the owners' wishes, all the buildings at Alexandria were made in the Gothic style. Work began with the Cottage palace

and Menelaws finished decorating it in 1829, The compact, almost square three-storey building with a roof painted the colour of straw was another reminder that this was a countryside dacha. The wrought iron grilles, balconies, bay-windows and terraces, the window frames and openings, and the moulding of the cornices were all in the English Gothic style. There was a touch of the Gothic too in the coloured glass at the tops of the bay-windows on the ground floor.By 1842 the palace was becoming cramped and Stakenschneider added a large dining-room and pantry with a balcony above and a marble terrace with a fountain.

The interior of the Cottage was exquisitely decorated. Perspective painting on the walls and ceiling, moulded friezes and cornices, extremely fine cast iron, carved oak and ash, complemented by pieces of "Gothic" furniture, porcelain, glass and bronze, created an atmosphere of cosiness that clearly hand "a woman's touch".

At Nicholas's request, the prominent German architect Karl Schinkel designed a Gothic church for Alexandria. This Chapel of St Alexander Nevsky was constructed in the western part of the park where its superb openwork silhouette splendidly accorded with the landscape.

The last palace to be built at Alexandria was the Lower Dacha. In 1895 Antony Tomishko constructed a pavilion with a tower topped by a belvedere on the shore of the gulf. When Nicholas II came to the throne, he asked the architect to enlarge the pavilion, turning it into a palace that was to become the residence of the last Romanov at Peterhof. An artificial harbour for the imperial yachts was constructed nearby. Until 1914 Nicholas spent the summers almost permanently here, but with the outbreak of the war the Romanovs left Peterhof for ever.

After the October Revolution of 1917 more than 19 palaces and pavilions at Peterhof became museums. During the Second World War the buildings were badly damaged, but the treasures evacuated and saved have made it possible to restore their former splendour.

Restoration work in the "capital of fountains" began soon after its liberation. The formal opening of the Lower Park took place on 17 June 1945. and the next year the first fountains came back to life. Today more than 150 fountains and four cascades are working at Peterhof, together with ten museums. Still the restoration work continues. The goal is not only to heal the wounds caused by the war, but also to return the parks to the appearance conceived by their creators.

1 <<
View of the Great Palace, the Upper
Garden and the Lower Park
The Upper Garden. Architects: JOHANN
FRIEDRICH BRAUNSTEIN, JEAN-BAPTISTE LE BLOND,
master gardeners: LEONARD HARNICHFELT,
A. BORISOV, 1714–24; architects: IVAN BLANK,
IVAN DAVYDOV, 1733–39
The Great Palace. Architects: JOHANN
FRIEDRICH BRAUNSTEIN, JEAN-BAPTISTE LE BLOND,
NICCOLO MICHETTI, 1714–25;
BARTOLOMEO FRANCESCO RASTRELLI, 1745–55,
ANDREI STAKENSCHNEIDER, 1847

2
Peterhof. The Upper Garden. The Neptune
Fountain. Sculptural group: *Neptune*.
Sculptors: CHRISTOPH RITTER, GEORG
SCHWEIGGER, JOHANN EILER; master founder:
WOLF HEROLD; medal-maker: J. WOHLRAB,
Nuremberg, 1650–69; sculptor:
BARTOLOMEO CARLO RASTRELLI, 1738
(mounted in 1799). Bronze

3
Peterhof. The Great Palace. The Armorial
Block. Architect: Bartolomeo Francesco
Rastrelli, 1750s

4
*Interior of the Church of SS Peter
and Paul in the Great Palace.* 1850
Watercolour by Eduard Hau

5
The Great Palace. The Main Staircase
Detail. Architect: Bartolomeo Francesco
Rastrelli, 1750s

7 >
The Great Palace. The Main Staircase
The upper landing

6 >
The Great Palace. The Main Staircase
Sculpture: *Autumn*. Gilded wood

8 <<
The Great Palace. The Picture Hall
Detail with a fireplace

9
The Great Palace. The Picture Hall
Architects: Jean-Baptiste Le Blond,
Niccolo Michetti, 1716–24; Jean-Baptiste
Vallin de La Mothe, 1764; painter: Pietro Rotari

10
The Great Palace. The Picture Hall
Fire-dog: *Venus*. Mid-18th century
France. Bronze

11
The Great Palace. The Ballroom
(Merchants' Room). Architect:
Bartolomeo Francesco Rastrelli, 1750s

12
The Great Palace
The Audience Hall. Architect:
Bartolomeo Francesco Rastrelli, 1750s

13 <<
The Great Palace. The Throne Room
Architects: Bartolomeo Francesco Rastrelli,
1750s; Yury Velten, 1777–78

16
The Great Palace. The Throne Room
Vigilius Erichsen. *Portrait of Catherine
the Great*. 1762. Oil on canvas

14
The Great Palace. The Throne Room
Heinrich Buchholtz. *Portrait of Catherine I*
Mid-18th century. Oil on canvas

15
The Great Palace. The Throne Room
Heinrich Buchholtz. *Portrait of Empress
Elizabeth Petrovna*. Mid-18th century
Oil on canvas

17
The Great Palace. The Chesme Hall
Architects: Bartolomeo Francesco Rastrelli,
1750s; Yury Velten, 1770s; painter:
Jakob Philip Hackaert, 1771–72

18
The Great Palace. The Cesme Hall
Jakob Philip Hackaert. *The Turkish Fleet
Retreating to the Chesme Bay.* 1771–72
Oil on canvas

19 >>
The Great Palace. The White Dining-Room
Architect: Bartolomeo Francesco Rastrelli,
1750s; Yury Velten, 1770s; The Husk
Service. 1768–74. Josiah Wedgwood's
Etruria Factory. Staffordshire, England
Faience, painted in monochrome
over a glaze

20
The Great Palace. The Eastern Chinese
Cabinet. Architect: Jean-Baptiste Vallin
de La Mothe, 1766–69

21
The Great Palace. Ceiling painting. 1769
Fiodor Vlasov (painting imitating porcelain)

22
The Great Palace. The Western Chinese
Cabinet. Architect: Jean-Baptiste Vallin
de La Mothe, 1766–69

23
The Great Palace
The Western Chinese Cabinet. Detail

24
The Great Palace. The Divan Room
Architects: Bartolomeo Francesco Rastrelli,
1750s; Yury Velten, 1770s

25 >
The Great Palace. The Partridge
Drawing-Room. Architects: Bartolomeo
Francesco Rastrelli, 1750s; Yury Velten, 1771

26
The Great Palace. The Standard (Passage)
Room. Architect: Bartolomeo Francesco
Rastrelli, 1750s

27
The Great Palace
The Dressing Room. Architect: Bartolomeo
Francesco Rastrelli, 1750s

28
The Great Palace. The Dressing Room
Unknown artist of the mid-18th century
Portrait of Grand Duke Piotr Fiodorovich
Oil on canvas

29
The Great Palace
The Large Blue Drawing-Room. Architect:
Bartolomeo Francesco Rastrelli, 1750s;
Andrei Stakenschneider, 1844

30
The Great Palace. The Crown Room
Architect: Bartolomeo Francesco Rastrelli,
1750s; Yury Velten, 1770

31
The Great Palace. The Oak Study
Architects: JEAN-BAPTISTE LE BLOND,
NICHOLAS PINEAU (carved panels), 1718–20

32
View of the Lower Park and the Voronikhin
Colonnade. Architect: Andrei Voronikhin;
sculptors: Ivan Martos, Ivan Prokofyev;
fountain master: Fiodor Strelnikov

33
Peterhof. The balustrade of the Upper
Grotto. Fountain: *Tritons*. 1801
Sculptor: Ivan Prokofyev

34 >>
Peterhof. View f the Avenue of Fountains
and the pool of the Great Cascade
Architects: Johann Friedrich Braunstein,
Jean-Baptiste Le Blond, Niccolo Michetti;
hydraulic engineer: Vasily Tuvolkov, 1715–24;
architect: Nikolai Benois, 1859–60

35 <
View of the Great Palace
and the Great Cascade
The Great Cascade. Architects: Johann
Friedrich Braunstein, Jean-Baptiste Le Blond,
Niccolo Michetti; Mikhail Zemtsov,
hydraulic engineer Vasily Tuvolkov,
fountain master: Paul Sualem, 1715–24;
sculptors: Ivan Martos, Ivan Prokofyev,
Mikhail Kozlovsky, Jean-Dominique Rachette,
Fedot Shubin, Feodosy Shchedrin, Fiodor
Gordeyev, Vasily Yekimov, Edmonde
Gastecloux, 1799–1806

36
The Great Cascade. Fountain sculptural
group: *Samson Rending Open the Jaws
of the Lion.* 1735. Sculptor Bartolomeo Carlo
Rastrelli. 1801. Cast by Mikhail Kozlovsky
Gilded bronze. Recreated by Vasily Simonov
and N. Mikhailov in 1947

37
The Great Cascade
The Eastern Cascade Stairway
Florentine Faun. 1800. Copy of an ancient
original of the 2nd century B.C.
Fountain vases. 1801–02. After a drawing
by ANDREI VORONIKHIN. Gilded bronze

38 >
The Great Cascade
The Eastern Cascade Stairway
Amazon. 1801. After a model by FIODOR
GORDEYEV. Copy of the original of
the 4th century B.C. Gilded bronze

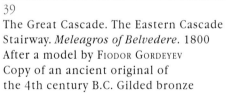

39
The Great Cascade. The Eastern Cascade
Stairway. *Meleagros of Belvedere*. 1800
After a model by Fiodor Gordeyev
Copy of an ancient original of
the 4th century B.C. Gilded bronze

40
The Great Cascade. The Eastern Cascade
Stairway. *Perseus*. 1801. After a model
by Feodosy Shchedrin. Gilded bronze

41
The Great Cascade. The Eastern Cascade
Stairway. *Ceres*. 1801. After a model
by Fiodor Gordeyev. From an ancient
original of the 4th century B.C.
Gilded bronze

42
The Great Cascade
The Western Cascade Stairway
Actaeon (centre). 1801. After
a model by Ivan Martos. Gilded bronze
Discobolus (right). 1800. Copy of
an ancient original of the 5th century
B.C. by Alcamenes. Gilded bronze
Capitoline Mercury. 1800. Copy of
an ancient original. Gilded bronze

43
The Great Cascade. The Western Cascade
Stairway. Site near the Lower Grotto
Capitoline Flora. 1800. Copy of
an ancient original. Gilded bronze
The Borghese Warrior (right). 1800
Master founders: EDMONDE GASTECLOUX,
VASILY YEKIMOV. A free copy of the original
by AGASIUS OF EPHESUS. 1st century B.C.

44
The Great Cascade
The Lower Grotto. The Lateral Hall
Pan and Olympus. 1857. Galvanoplastic
copy of an ancient original
Workshop of I. Hamburger,
St Petersburg. Gilded copper

45
The Great Cascade. The Lower Grotto
The Lateral Hall. Mascaron decorating
the key-stone over the arch of the Lower
Grotto. 1723. Gilded bronze

46
The central part of the Lower Park
Eastern parterre

47
The central area of the Lower Park
The Fountains of the Marble Benches.
Fountain: *Nymph*. Architect: ANDREI
STAKENSCHNEIDER, 1854. From an ancient
original of the 2nd century B.C.
Gilded bronze

48 >
The central area of the Lower Park
The Fountains of the Marble Benches
Fountain: *Danaid*. Architect: ANDREI
STAKENSCHNEIDER, sculptor: IVAN VITALI,
1854, copy of the original by CHRISTIAN
DANIEL RAUCH. Gilded bronze

49
The Adam Fountain
Architect: NICCOLO MICHETTI, 1722;
sculptor: GIOVANNI BONAZZA, 1718. Marble

50 >
The Eva Fountain. Architects: NICCOLO MICHETTI,
Timofei Usov, 1726; sculptor: GIOVANNI
BONAZZA, 1718. Marble

51
The Lion Cascade.
Architect: NICCOLO MICHETTI, 1799–1800;
ANDREI STAKENSCHNEIDER, 1854–57
Serdobolye granite (colonnade)

52
The Lion Cascade. Mascaron. 1850s. Cast-iron

53 >>
The Roman Fountains
Architects: IVAN BLANK, IVAN DAVYDOV, 1738–39;
BARTOLOMEO FRANCESCO RASTRELLI, 1756;
1800 (reconstructed)

55
The Sun Fountain
Architects: Niccolo Michetti, 1721–24;
Yury Velten, I. Yakovlev, 1770s

56
The Pyramid Fountain
Architects: Niccolo Michetti, Johann Friedrich
Braunstein, Mikhail Zemtsov, 1721–1724
fountain masters: P. Sualem; I. Yakovlev,
fountain master: Fiodor Strelnikov, 1799

54 <<
The Monplaisir Garden. Trick fountain:
Little Oak. Sculptor: Bartolomeo Carlo
Rastrelli, 1735; fountain master:
Fiodor Strelnikov, 1802

57
The Golden Hill Cascade
Architects: NICCOLO MICHETTI, 1721–23;
MIKHAIL ZEMTSOV, 1731–32;
NIKOLAI BENOIS, 1870

58
The Triton Cloche Fountain
Architect: JOHANN FRIEDRICH BRAUNSTEIN, 1721

59
The Chessboard Hill Cascade
(Dragon Hill). Architects: Niccolo Michetti,
1721; Mikhail Zemtsov, Ivan Blank,
Ivan Davydov, 1737–39

60
The Dragon Cascade (The Chessboard Hill)
Dragon. By Hans Konradt Ossner. 1738–39
Painted bronze

61
The Orangery Garden. The Great Orangery
Architects: Johann Friedrich Braunstein,
Mikhail Zemtsov, 1722–25; to a design
by Niccolo Michetti

62 >
The Orangery Garden. The Orange
Fountain. 1726. After a model by Carlo
Bartolomeo Rastrelli. Gilded bronze

63
The Hermitage Pavilion. The Hall
(The Dining-Room). Faience tableware
First half of the 18th century. Delft,
Holland, Germany

64
The Hermitage Pavilion. The Kitchen

65 >
The Hermitage Pavilion. Architect:
JOHANN FRIEDRICH BRAUNSTEIN, 1721–25

66
The western area of the Lower Park
View of the Marly Palace

67 >
The Marly Palace
Architect: Johann Friedrich Braunstein, 1720–23

68 <
The Marly Palace. The Entrance Hall

69
The Marly Palace. The Oak Study
First quarter of the 18th century
Germany. Oak, ivory inlay

70
The Marly Palace. The Library. Globe
First half of the 18th century. England

71
The Palace of Monplaisir. Architects:
Johann Friedrich Braunstein, Jean-Baptiste
Le Blond, Niccolo Michetti, 1714–23

72
The Monplaisir Garden
The Cloche Fountain. *Faun and a Kid*
1817. Sculptor: Ivan Martos. Gilded bronze
1723. Architect: Niccolo Michetti (pedestal)

73 >>
The Palace of Monplaisir
The Western Gallery

75
The Palace of Monplaisir. The Hall

76
The Palace of Monplaisir. The Hall
ADAM SILO. *Ships Riding at Anchor*
Oil on canvas

74 <<
The Palace of Monplaisir. The Maritime Study

77
The Palace of Monplaisir
The Secretary's Room
Jacob Torenvliet. *Breakfast.* Oil on canvas

78
The Palace of Monplaisir. The Hall
Abraham Stork. *Landing Stage in a Town*
Oil on canvas

79 >>
The Palace of Monplaisir. The Hall. Detail

80 <
The Palace of Monplaisir. The Bedroom

82 >
The Palace of Monplaisir. The Kitchen

81 >
The Palace of Monplaisir. The Kitchen. Detail

84
The Palace of Monplaisir. The Lacquer Study
Architect: Johann Friedrich Braunstein, 1720–22

83 <
The Palace of Monplaisir
The Lacquer Study. The Chimney

85
The Catherine Block. Architects:
Bartolomeo Francesco Rastrelli, 1747–48;
Giacomo Quarenghi, 1785–86
The Monplaisir Garden. The Sheaf
Fountain. Architects: Niccolo Michetti,
F. Isakov, 1722–23

86
The Catherine Block
The Study of Alexander I

87 >>
The Catherine Block
The Yellow Hall

88
Alexandria. The Cottage Palace
Architect: ADAM MENELAWS, 1826–29

89
View of the Cottage. 1854
Watercolour by JOSEPH CHARLEMAGNE

90
The Cottage Palace. The Small Study

91
The Cottage Palace. The Drawing-Room

92
The Cottage Palace. The Library

93
The Cottage Palace
The Study of Empress Maria Fiodorovna
1896–97. Architect: ROBERT MELZER

TSARSKOYE SELO

"**W**e're going to Tsarskoye Selo" — that line of verse from Osip Mandelstam might serve as epigraph to this town since, from the eighteenth century onwards, year after year hosts of people have hastened to this small suburb of St Petersburg to visit its palaces and stroll in its parks.

Romantic tales, art and poetry bring life to these places: the imagination of every era is stirred by images of the past. All styles of art found reflection here — the picturesque forms of the Baroque, the harmonious beauty of Classicism, the heavenward striving of the Neo-Gothic, Eastern exoticism in buildings featuring Chinese and Turkish motifs.

Today the Tsarskoye Selo ensemble if one of the richest treasure-houses of Russian artistic culture. Three parks, covering a territory of 600 hectares, contain more than a hundred architectural edifices from grandiose palaces and great historical monuments to intimate pavilions and a variety of bridges crossing the waterways.

The history of the creation of the palace-and-park complex goes back to the early eighteenth century, to the time when the lands around the Baltic coast were being reclaimed and developed. In 1710 Peter the Great presented this area to his wife Catherine (1684–1727) and in 1717 she had the first masonry palace "with 16 lights" constructed here on the top of a hill. It was intended as a place to rest after hunting in the dense surrounding forests. The chosen site was known in Finnish as "saari mois" — "elevated spot", in Russian this became Saarskaya Myza (manor) and later Sarskoye Selo (village). The place was transformed into the grand suburban residence of Tsarskoye Selo (literally Tsar's Village) under Peter and Catherine's daughter Empress Elizabeth (1709–1761).

The main element in the magnificent complex of buildings at Tsarskoye Selo was the tremendous Catherine Palace stretching for a length of 306 metres. The sky-blue walls, gilded domes, wrought-iron grilles and highly expressive sculpture on the façade all combined to make a vivid, unforgettable impression. At any time of year, but especially on a dull winter's day, in the pale light of the St Petersburg sun, the walls of the Catherine Palace seem to radiate a joyful energy, giving a charge to all the surrounding area and filling it with a radiant feeling of happiness.

Between 1744 and 1756 thousands of labourers and craftsmen working to the designs of the architects Mikhail Zemtsov (1686–1743), Alexei Kvasov, Savva Chevakinsky and later Bartolomeo Francesco Rastrelli (1700–1771) constructed a place building in the Baroque style. Its decoration was the work of celebrated Italian artists, other European experts and, alongside them, hundreds of skilled Russian: woodcarvers and stonemasons, gilders, chasers, painters, stucco plasterers, smiths and other unknown masters.

In July 1756 the palace was opened for foreign guests and from that time on grand receptions became a tradition here. The state rooms are located on the second storey and comprise the Golden Enfilade connected by a corridor that is strung with a series of magnificent gilded portals marking the entrances into the palace's richest interiors. Rastrelli employed a variety of artistic techniques in the decoration of these halls in order to give each interior its own distinctive, original appearance.

The grandest hall of the Golden Enfilade is the Great (or Throne) Hall which was used for official ceremonies. In the eighteenth century it was known as "the Bright Gallery" on account of its elongated shape and the large number of windows bringing in light from both the garden and the courtyard sides. The main decorative elements in the hall are gilded carving and mirrors that concealed the length of the walls, creating the illusion of the carved décor being in motion, a lively play of light and shade. Placed above the windows were gilded carved figures of semi-

recumbent "ladies" and seated putti, fluttering as it were, in the streams of whimsical carving. A unique acoustic effect has been created in the hall — even a weak sound echoes several times off the walls due to the fact that hollow spaces have been carved out inside the sculptures that act as resonators. This little secret of the hall was devised by the architect Rastrelli and was a very successful innovation during crowded receptions.

The best known rooms in the palace include the Amber Room created in 1755. The chief element in its decoration are mosaic panels made from pieces of amber with a great variety of sizes and shades. These panels were presented to Peter the Great in 1716 by King Frederick William I of Prussia. (Germans had long been masters at the artistic working of amber gathered on the shores of the Baltic.) The Amber Room contained caskets, carved snuffboxes, chess and draughts sets and goblets all made of amber by the craftsmen of Danzig and presented to the Russian court by German kings and electors. Somewhat later, at Empress Elizabeth's request, Rastrelli gave the room mirror pilasters, a ceiling painting, a patterned parquet floor and gilded light sources — wall lamps in the form of parrots perching on branches. This unique interior was soon being celebrated as the Eighth Wonder of the World.

The picture gallery is adorned by 130 works produced by prominent Western European artists. The Dutch, Flemish, Italian, German and French works were purchased in 1745 specially for this room and installed its the north and south walls. The landscapes and still lifes, architectural views and portraits, mythological and biblical scenes were created by Jean Marc Nattier, Jacques Blanchard, Emmanuel de Witte, Adriaen van Ostade, David Teniers and others. The paintings are placed right next to each other, separated only by narrow frames, and cover the entire surface of the two walls like a tapestry. This was the customary way of displaying paintings in Europe before the nineteenth century. Rastrelli arranged the paintings symmetrically around the large tiled stoves in the centre of the walls in a deliberately decorative manner.

The elegant rooms of the Golden Enfilade follow each other in a grand succession, embodying the artistic tastes of the day and incorporating a host of splendid works of art. The State, Small and Cavaliers' Dining-Rooms. the drawing-rooms known as the Crimson and Green Pilaster Rooms, the Portrait Hall and the Antechambers were permanently filled with guests attending receptions, dinners, masquerades and balls.

The palace owed its origins to two women who occupied the Russian throne, Catherine I and Elizabeth, while it flourished under a third, Catherine II (1729–1796). During her reign Tsarskoye Selo would become the permanent seat of the Russian court during the summer months. Talented architects working in the Classical style — Yury Velten (1730–1801), Antonio Rinaldi (1709–1794), Vasily Neyelov (1724–1782), Ilya Neyelov (1745–1793), Charles Cameron (1743–1812) and Giacomo Quarenghi (1744–1817) between them made considerable alterations and additions to the established architectural ensemble.

The Zubov Wing of the palace, added in the 1770s, contained the personal apartments of Catherine the Great, while in the northern part of the building rooms were constructed for her son Paul (1754–1801). Both sets of apartments were finished in the Classical style that was founded on the traditions of Ancient Greek and Roman art. Different colours and different ornaments appeared in the interiors of the Green Dining-Room, the State and Blue Drawing-Rooms. In the smaller, cosy apartments glitter and opulence gave way to refined simplicity. gilded woodcarving gave way to stucco mouldings.

The Green Dining-Room has one of the most original interiors in this suite. The décor, devised by the Scottish architect Charles Cameron, reminds one of the cameo ware produced by the Wedgwood company in England that was popular in the later eighteenth century. The light green walls are embellished with white moulded reliefs in the form of garlands of foliage, vases and architectural ornaments. Between these are relief images of youths and girls in ancient costumes, medallions featuring playful cupids and multi-figure scenes inspired by the myths of Phaeton, Poseidon and Hermes. The painted white chairs with green upholstery and the bronze articles by the marble fireplace were also produced to Cameron's designs specially for the Green Dining-Room. Despite its name, tables were only brought into this room at meal times.

At the end of the eighteenth century Catherine the Great gave orders for the construction of a new block alongside the Great Palace for her numerous grandchildren — the sons and daughters of Paul and Maria Fiodorovna. Later this four-storey building accommodated the Lyceum, the elite school that numbered the great Russian poet Pushkin among its first pupils. On the south side of the palace Charles Cameron erected a remarkable architectural complex of a highly original kind inspired by Roman *thermae* (public baths). The architect combined in an integral whole the Cold Baths and Agate Rooms, the adjoining gallery, the Hanging Garden that linked these structures with part of the Great Palace and the gently sloping Ramp descending to the park. This enabled Catherine to move around the palace halls and the alleys of the park in a Bath chair. The Empress was especially fond of the open gallery bearing Cameron's name that was intended as a place to stroll. Placed within its Ionic colonnade were busts of famous men: ancient philosophers and great military commanders.

At the same time as the palace was being constructed a regular park was laid out running from its southern façade. Rastrelli's fertile imagination dictated the appearance in the park of trellised arbours, bosquets and a parterre enhanced by marble sculptures, elaborately trimmed trees and bushes, trees in tubs and clear ponds. All these were symbols of the endless summer court festivities of Empress Elizabeth's time. With time the regular park came to be known as the Old Garden.

One of the parks attractions was the buildings constructed there in the mid-eighteenth century. At the opposite end of the central alley from the palace there still stands Rastrelli's remarkable Hermitage. This truly isolated building was completed at the same time as the Great Palace in 1756. Its sky-blue façades adorned by white columns and moulded details captured the attention at a distance. The walls of the main hall and four cabinets are covered with gilded carving, painting and mirrors. A lifting mechanism raised the tables laid with viands to the hall above, permitting the diners to dispense with the presence of servants.

The Grotto Pavilion, a second park building from Elizabeth's time, was intended as a place to rest during boat rides. Rastrelli conceived this pavilion, surrounded on three sides by the waters of the Great Pond, as the realm of the sea god Neptune as is shown by the allegorical figures of dolphins, the depictions of sea monsters, shells and plants in the capitals of the columns, above the windows and the entrance portal. Here, by the pond, the older, regular, part of the park ended and the new landscape park that sought to imitate the natural world began.

Catherine the Great changed the layout of the Tsarskoye Selo park. In the 1770s, on expansive meadows extending from the shores of the man-made Great Pond, her court architect Vasily Neyelov and the master-gardeners Joseph Busch and Trifon Ilyin installed picturesque pavilions and bowers, with a variety of functions and styles. This resulted in the appearance of the Upper and Lower Bathhouses, and also the construction, in keeping with English fashion of the day, of the Tower Ruin designed by Velten, the Pyramid (Vasily Neyelov and Cameron), the Concert Hall (Quarenghi), the Marble Bridge and Admiralty (Vasily Neyelov). The Chesme Column rose majestically from the smooth surface of the pond, designed by Rinaldi to mark the victory in the Russo-Turkish War of 1768–74.

Between 1792 and 1796, not far from the Catherine Palace, Giacomo Quarenghi constructed the magnificent Alexander (or New) Palace. This was a wedding present from a doting grandmother, Catherine II, to her beloved grandson, the future Alexander I (1777–1825). Its architecture in the Russian Clas-

sical style contrasted strongly with the opulent Baroque edifices of the previous era. The building harmonizes astonishingly well with the surrounding landscape park that also came to bear Alexander's name. The palace is an elegant two-storey structure with twin wings either side of the main block and a splendid double Corinthian colonnade that creates the palace's strikingly majestic image. The walls inside the new palace were faced with artificial marble and divided by arcades, a feature dictated by the austere simplicity of the interior décor. Alexander and his bride Yelizaveta Alexeyevna (1779–1826) were delighted with their new palace, but did not live there for long. Catherine's death in 1796, the succession of his father Paul, the move to the Mikhailovsky Castle and the war with Napoleon all kept Alexander I in constant motion. Nevertheless, he brought the palaces, orangeries and parks to the peak of condition. "I manage more in one day at Tsarskoye Selo than in a whole week in St Petersburg," the Emperor confessed in his writings. Despite the fact that Alexander spent little time in his Tsraskoye Selo palaces, he had work carried out to reconstruct parts of the Catherine Palace that had suffered from fire in 1820. The task was entrusted to Vasily Stasov (1769–1848) and it was to that architect's designs that the State (Marble) Study of Alexander I, the Marble (Stasov) Staircase and the Stasov Hall (Church Anteroom) were created.

The Alexander Park, originally laid out in the 1720s, underwent many changes in keeping with the changing artistic tastes of the later eighteenth and nineteenth centuries. The squares of the old regular garden that flanked the Triple Alley still retain their original names: the Mushroom Courtine, Little Lakes, Mount Parnassus, the Chinese Theatre. This old, formerly regular, part of the garden is fringed by the Krestovy Canal. Here some splendid bridges designed by Cameron have survived: the Large Chinese, Dragon and two Small Chinese Bridges. Another architect, Vasily Neyelov, enhanced the exquisite curve of the Krestovy Canal with his Krestovy Bridge crowned by a pavilion in the shape of an elegant Chinese house. Four spans in the form of flights of marble steps lead to the pavilion and from it to the square by the Catherine Palace and to the Chinese Village constructed in 1782–96 to the designs of Charles Cameron. The village's broad streets are flanked by houses in the Chinese style with tall painted roofs. The streets lead to a square from which a pagoda rises. The houses were intended as places where honoured visitors to Tsarskoye Selo could take rest.

The landscape area of the Alexander Park was embellished by pavilions designed by the architect Adam Menelaws (1753–1831). Their architecture reflected a fascination with the Middle Ages typical of early-nineteenth-century Romanticism. The White Tower guarded by cast-iron lions and knights; the Chapelle tower surrounded by artificial ruins, the Arsenal that housed a collection of antique weaponry, and the Pensionary Stables where the imperial steeds lived out their days all gave this part of the park a distinctive romantic character.

The Alexander Palace became a home for the imperial family under Nicholas I (1796–1855), Alexander's brother and successor. From the outset of this tsar's reign, his family moved here in early spring and remained in the palace, with intermissions, until late into the autumn. They lived a secluded existence in the Alexander Palace, while official receptions, grand festivities and church services were from this time held in the Catherine Palace. It was Nicholas I who established the tradition of resting at Tsarskoye Selo from the numerous, exhausting receptions, social gatherings and balls. Horace Vernet's painting *The Tsarskoye Selo Carousel*, created in 1843 on the occasion of the Golden Wedding of Nicholas I and Alexander Fiodorovna, depicts the whole happy family in a jolly festive cavalcade against the background of the Alexander Park.

By the reign of Emperor Alexander II (1818–1881), the residence at Tsarskoye Selo had become a tremendous ensembles of palaces and parks that was the setting for the summer life of the Russian Empire. The private rooms in the Zubov Wing of the Catherine Palace became the young Tsar's favourite retreat. They were situated on the ground floor and looked out onto the Private Garden with its colonnade (pergola) in the Italian style, fountain and flowerbed. This garden was used only by members of the imperial family. The garden was laid out by the court architect Alexander Vidov (1829–1896) in keeping with the owners' tastes.

In Alexander II's time there were reconstructions not only in the park, but in the Catherine Palace as well. The Main Staircase situated in the centre of the building was created in 1860 to the design of Hippolyto Monighetti (1818–1878) who chose Rococo stylization reminiscent of the carved decoration of Rastrelli's interiors. The balcony railings are embellished with the gilded monograms of Alexander II and his consort Maria Alexandrovna. They spent the best years of their lives here. It was to Tsarskoye Selo that Alexander II returned from the coronation in Moscow that formally marked the beginning of a new era associated with his name. He often met with like-minded people in the Catherine Palace to discuss questions relating to the great reforms of his reign.

Emperor Alexander III (1845-1894) chose the right wing of the Alexander Palace for family sojourns, while the Catherine Palace was allotted the role of formal residence intended for official receptions. The interiors of the private rooms contained paintings by Russian artists from the Emperor's personal collection, a host of family photographs, gifts and tributes.

The last Russian Emperor, Nicholas II (1868–1918), was born in the Alexander Palace at Tsarskoye Selo. The Catherine Palace with its exquisite interiors and rich collections had a special meaning for Nicholas: the history of the palace was part of his family history. The palace was a setting for all the jubilee celebrations of the early twentieth century: the 200th anniversary of St Petersburg in 1903; the 200th anniversary of the victory at Poltava in 1909; the 200th anniversary of Tsarskoye Selo in 1910; the Tsarskoye Selo Jubilee Exhibition in 1911; the 300th anniversary of the Romanov Dynasty in 1913.

These celebrations were attended by the highest dignitaries of the empire, ambassadors, European crowned heads and relatives of the imperial family who occupied high posts in the state. In the early years of the twentieth century the guards regiments founded by Peter the Great celebrated their own jubilees one after another. Again the Catherine Palace hosted the celebrations. The festivities began with a grand church service which was followed by a parade on the palace parade ground, a formal reception in the Great Hall for the officers and their retinues, a banquet for the lower ranks on the ground floor.

The Emperor and his family lived permanently in the left wing of the Alexander Palace. The Palisander Drawing-Room, Lilac Study, State Study of Nicholas II and Maple Drawing-Room were created by the Melzer company to designs by Robert (Roman) Melzer in the then-fashionable Art Nouveau style. The main criteria for the arrangement of the rooms were comfort and convenience. All the technological innovations of the day were incorporated: electricity, telephones, a lift. For the children one of the rooms was adapted to make a cinema and a projector installed. But the warmth of human contact was more important than the fashionable décor of the palace halls. "Faith, Hope and Love — that is all that matters," Empress Alexandra Fiodorovna was fond of saying. This phrase perfectly characterizes relations within this friendly and loving family. They were sticklers for tradition: things introduced in the palaces under Catherine the Great were still part of everyday life in the early twentieth century. The parquet floors were polished with the same wax; new gilded furniture was upholstered in silk with patterns in the style of the eighteenth century. The air in the living apartments was scented with the same herbs. Footmen and messengers bustled about them dressed in gold-embroidered kaftans and feathered hats. Moors in white turbans and red pantaloons stood by the doors awaiting instructions. The whole impression was that for over a century time had stood still here.

Yet at that same time, in 1906, close to the palace, the architect Danini was constructing the first garage for four cars belonging to Nicholas II. The Emperor took a keen interest in the technical advances of his time. Automobiles were specially commissioned for him from German and British companies. Even his heir, Alexis, had his own child's car which he drove around the palace halls. In 1913 the engineer Miniayev erected a large modern hangar with a glazed roof to house not four, but forty cars. Car rides are recorded on many of the photographs taken by members of the imperial family themselves. Photography was another of the Romanovs' enthusiasms. Every member of the family, included Alexis and the girls, had a personal camera with which they recorded their daily lives.

The Alexander Palace is closely connected with the final days of the Romanov dynasty. It was here, following tumultuous historical events, that on 2 April 1917, Nicholas II, having already abdicated, wrote in his diary: "The Glorious Resurrection of Christ. Before breakfast I exchanged Easter greetings with all the servants... There were 135 people altogether." This was the last festival the family

celebrated in their home. The further history of the palaces and parks of Tsarskoye Selo did not involve the Romanovs.

After the October Revolution of 1917, museums of history and art were established in the palaces of Tsarskoye Selo, becoming one of the most significant cultural centres in the country.

When war broke out with Nazi Germany in 1941 the extremely precious collections of the Tsarskoye Selo museums had to be evacuated to the rear of the country, to Novosibirsk, Sarapul and Nizhny Novgorod. In the first two months of the war, 20,000 exhibits were dispatched, while the park sculpture was buried in the ground. The 28-month enemy occupation of the town — from 17 September 1941 to 24 January 1944 — left the palaces and park structure substantially destroyed. Recreating them from the ruins demanded tremendous efforts, and for over fifty years now the museum workers, experts in various fields of restoration, architects, art historians, artists, sculptors, woodcarvers, gilders, gardeners, land improvers and other specialists have been labouring to bring back the lost treasures of Tsarskoye Selo.

In 1959 the first six restored interiors in the Catherine Palace were opened to the public. At present the museum display consists of 26 restored rooms, including the state rooms of the Golden Enfilade, the private rooms of the future Paul I, and a few interiors that relate to Alexander I.

The most expensive, laborious and difficult project has been the restoration of the decoration of the Amber Room. The decision to recreate this interior was taken in 1979, as all efforts to find the original panels looted and hidden by the Nazi occupiers had failed. A special programme was developed to reproduce the old technique of working amber and to study techniques of amber carving. It drew on the experience of restoring objects from the museum's collection of amber decorative and applied art that spans the sixteenth to twentieth centuries and numbers some 100 items. They provided direct parallels for the restorers in their work to recreate the lost panels. Of great use were pre-war photographs of the interior, old technical drawings, archive descriptions and the recollections of witnesses. Thorough studies were made of small broken fragments of the amber décor: mouldings, flat "patchwork", tiny elements of carving, some 70 scraps in all. Only after experience had been built up by accomplishing this highly complex work were the team able to move on to recreating the amber panels. This work is at present being brought to a successful conclusion after twenty years of intensive labour with the financial support of the German company Ruhrgas AG in time for the 300th anniversary of the foundation of St Petersburg. Viewing the amber mosaic panels decorated with carved ornament from the same material already installed on the walls and the Florentine mosaics of semiprecious stones, it is possible to state that they are of artistic value in their own right. There is no doubt that this unique piece of work evokes astonishment and admiration despite the fact that it has been produced by late-twentieth-century craftsmen and differs from the lost original.

The fate of the Alexander Palace took a different turn after the war. It was not reopened as a museum and the collections that had been saved were dispersed to many other museums. Up until the 1990s, the famous palace was perceived only as a beautiful decoration in the park. (Since 1951 the building has housed a classified naval institution.) Until recently only a few people knew that within the palace the authentic interiors of the suite of state rooms and a few rooms in living apartments belonging to the family of the last Russian Tsar had survived.

In August 1997 a new chapter opened in the 200-year history of this remarkable edifice: a display opened in the left wing of the building, where part of the décor of the private apartments still exists, under the title "Reminiscences in the Alexander Palace". The opening of this exhibition was one of the symbolic events in Russian history over the past decade when it at last became possible to present the full history of the imperial palaces with-

<< YEGOR MEYER
The Garden Façade of the New (Alexander) Palace. 1840s
Oil on canvas

HORACE VERNET
Merry-Go-Round at Tsarskoye Selo. 1843. Oil on canvas

ERNST LIPHART
Portrait of Emperor Nicholas II. 1900. Oil on canvas

out the interference of censorship. The restored interiors bring to life extremely interesting pages in the country's history and the life of the ruling dynasty, visibly embodied in the decoration and the unique art collections. Thanks to the restoration work that still continues in the twenty-first century, the palaces of Tsarskoye Selo are not silent monuments of yesteryear, but a living link between present and past. And so the lines that Pushkin wrote when banished to his family's country estate — "The whole world is foreign to us. Our homeland is Tsarskoye Selo" — remain relevant even today. We are reminded of them by the monument to the poet created by the sculptor Robert Bach and installed in the Lyceum Garden close to the Tsarskoye Selo palaces.

94 <<
Tsarskoye Selo. The Catherine Palace
and the regular park

95 <
The Catherine Palace. The park façade
Architects: ANDREI KVASOV, SAVVA CHEVAKINSKY,
BARTOLOMEO FRANCESCO RASTRELLI, 1744–56

96 <
The Great Palace at Tsarskoye Selo. 1755–61
Engraving, after a drawing by MIKHAIL MAKHAYEV
Artists: P. ARTEMYEV, E. VNUKOV, N. CHELNAKOV

97
The Catherine Palace
Detail of the park façade. Atlantes

98
The Catherine Palace
Sculpture: *Glory*
Early 18th century. Venice
Sculptor: ALVISE TAGLIAPIETRA.
Marble

99
The Catherine Palace
The upper landing of the Marble Staircase

100 >
The Catherine Palace
The Main (Marble) Staircase
Architect: Hippolyto Monighetti, 1860

101
The Catherine Palace
The Great Hall (Throne Room). 1750s
Architect: Bartolomeo Francesco Rastrelli

102
*The Third Antechamber in the Great Palace
at Tsarskoye Selo.* 1865. Watercolour
by A. H. Kolb

103 >>
The Catherine Palace. The Great Hall
(Throne Room). Detail

104
The Catherine Palace. The White Dining-
Room. Architect: Bartolomeo Francesco
Rastrelli, 1750s

105
The Catherine Palace
The White Dining-Room. Items from
a service in the "Japanese taste". 1740s
The Meissen Porcelain Factory

106
The Catherine Palace
The White Dining-Room. Detail

107
The Catherine Palace
The White Dining-Room
Stand. 18th century. West Europe
Items of the "common" service
Last quarter of the 18th century
The Imperial Porcelain Factory,
St Petersburg

108
The Catherine Palace. The Dining-Room
of Cavaliers-in-Attendance. Architect:
Bartolomeo Francesco Rastrelli, 1750s

109
The Catherine Palace. The Dining-Room
for Cavaliers-in-Attendance. The mount
of a mirror frame and stove

110
The Catherine Palace. The Crimson Room
1750s. Architect: Bartolomeo Francesco Rastrelli

111
The Catherine Palace. The Green Room
1750s. Architect: Bartolomeo Francesco Rastrelli

112 <<
The Catherine Palace
The suite of state rooms (the "Golden Enfilade"). View from the Crimson Room
Architect: BARTOLOMEO FRANCESCO RASTRELLI, 1750s

113
The Catherine Palace. The Portrait Hall
Architect: BARTOLOMEO FRANCESCO RASTRELLI, 1750s

114
The Catherine Palace. The Portrait Hall. IVAN ADOLSKY. *Portrait of Empress Catherine I with a Black Boy.* After 1725

118 >
The Catherine Palace. The Amber Room
Architect: Bartolomeo Francesco Rastrelli,
1755 (the interior is being recreated)

116
The Catherine Palace. The Amber Room
Detail of the panel with an amber frame
and the Florentine mosaic *Sight*. 1750s

115
The Catherine Palace. The Amber Room
Detail of the panel with an amber frame
and the Florentine mosaic *Sight*

117 >
The Catherine Palace. The Amber Room
Detail of the panel with an amber frame

119 <
The Catherine Palace. The Amber Room
Florentine mosaic: *Sense of Touch
and Sense of Smell*

120
The Catherine Palace. The Amber Room
Candelabrum-clock in the form of a tree
with a pastoral scene. About 1750
Paris. Gilded bronze, iron,
porcelain and enamels

121 <<
The Catherine Palace
The Picture Hall. Detail with the door
portal of the southern wall

122
The Catherine Palace. The Picture Hall
Architect: Bartolomeo Francesco Rastrelli, 1750s

123
The Catherine Palace
The Picture Hall. Caryatid

124
The Catherine Palace
Clock: *Peace and Abundance*
1770. Paris; by J.-L. Prière,
after a drawing by François
Boucher; the clock mechanism
by A. Peltier. Bronze, cast,
chased, gilded and patinated

125 <
The Catherine Palace
The Green Dining-Room
Serving table

126
The Catherine Palace
The Green Dining-Room
Architect: Charles Cameron, 1780s

127
The Catherine Palace
The Green Dining-Room. The suite
of rooms in the apartments of Grand
Duke Pavel Petrovich and his wife
Maria Fiodorovna

128 <
The Catherine Palace
The Blue Drawing-Room. Fireplace

129
The Catherine Palace
The Blue Drawing-Room
Architect: CHARLES CAMERON, 1780s

130 <
The Catherine Palace.
The Blue Drawing-Room
IVAN NIKITIN. *Portrait of Emperor
Peter the Great.* About 1722
Oil on canvas

131
The Catherine Palace
The Blue Chinese Drawing-Room
Architect: Charles Cameron, 1780s

132
The Catherine Palace
The Blue Chinese Drawing-Room
Georg Christoph Grooth. *Portrait
of Empress Elizabeth Petrovna as Flora,
the Goddess of Flowers*. 1748–49
Oil on copper-plate

133
The Catherine Palace. The Choir Anteroom
Architect: CHARLES CAMERON, 1780s; decor
of the 1840s

134
The Catherine Palace. The Choir
Anteroom. Detail of upholstery. 1771
After a drawing by PHILIPPE DE LASSALLE
Silk and chenille

135
The Catherine Palace. The Bedchamber
Architect: Charles Cameron, 1780s

136
The Catherine Palace
The Bedchamber. Fireplace

137 >>
The Catherine Palace
The Bedchamber. Sculpture: *Cupid*
Sculptor: Nicolas-François Gillet

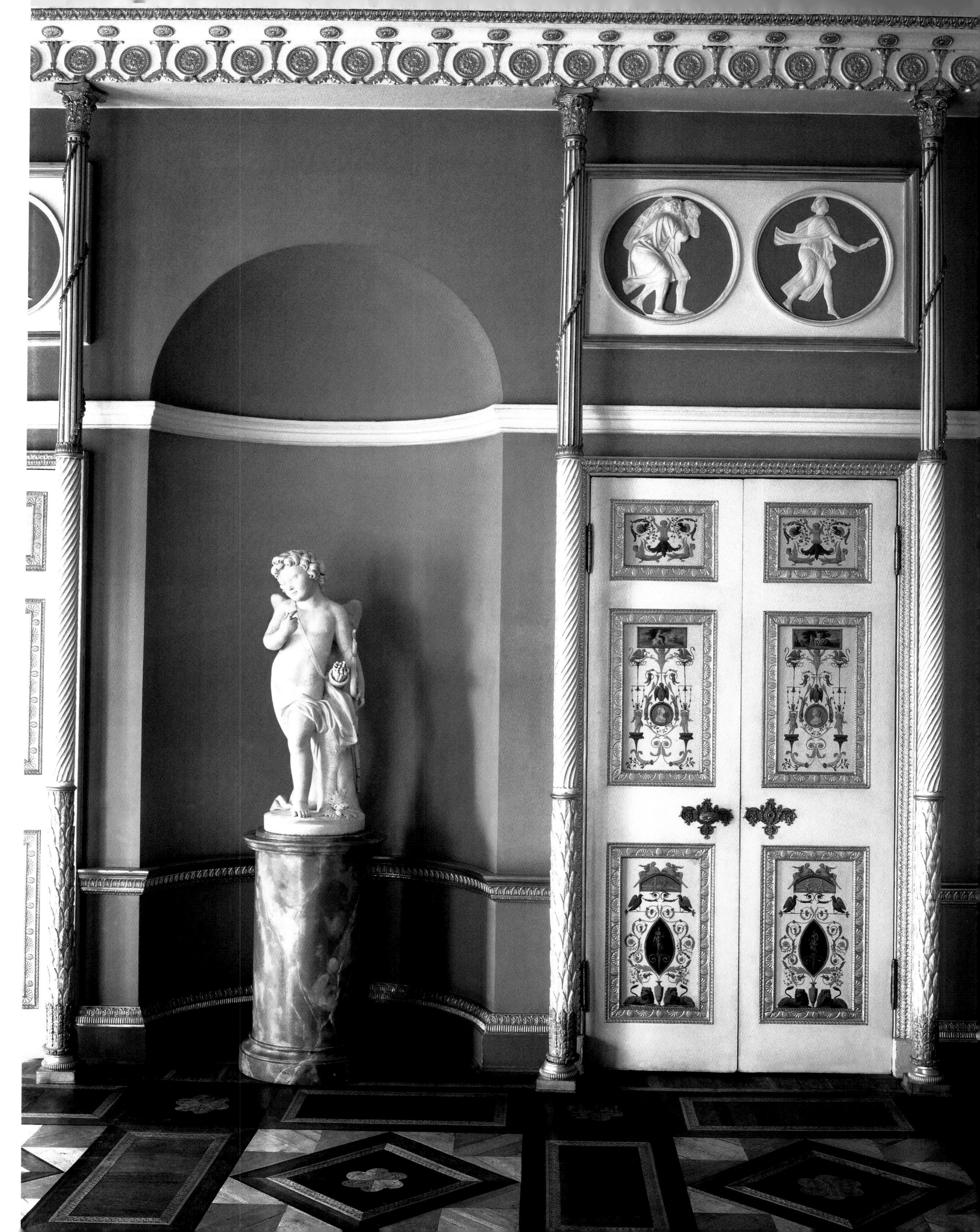

138
The Catherine Palace
The Marble Study of Emperor Alexander I
Architect: Vasily Stasov, 1820

139
The Catherine Palace. The Marble Study
of Emperor Alexander I. Table ink set
First quarter of the 19th century
After drawings by Vasily Stasov
Malachite and bronze

140
The Catherine Palace. The State (Marble)
Study of Emperor Alexander I. 1815
Portret of the imperor Alexander I
Watercolour by Jean-Baptiste Ichabey

141
The Catherine Park. Parterre

142
Friedrich Hartmann Barisien
View of the Old Garden at Tsarskoye Selo and Sadovaya Street. 1760. Oil on canvas

143 >>
The Catherine Palace. The Church of the Resurrection of Christ. Architects:
Savva Chevakinsky, Bartolomeo Francesco Rastrelli, 1745–56

144
The Catherine Park. The Upper Bath
Pavilion. Architect: Ilya Neyelov, 1777–79

145
The Catherine Park. The Hermitage
Pavilion. Architects: ANDREI KVASOV,
MIKHAIL ZEMTSOV, SAVVA CHEVAKINSKY,
BARTOLOMEO FRANCESCO RASTRELLI, 1744–56

146
The Hermitage in the Park at Tsarskoye Selo
1759. After a drawing by MIKHAIL MAKHAYEV,
engraved by ALEXEI GREKOV

147
The Catherine Park
The Cameron Gallery. View of the façade
from the Maids-of-Honour (Flower) Garden

148
The Catherine Park. The Cameron Gallery
Architect: Charles Cameron, 1782–86

149
The Catherine Park
The Cameron Gallery. The Colonnade
or the Gallery for Promenades. Busts
1790s. The St Petersburg Academy of Arts
Cast by EDMONDE GASTECLOUX. Copies from
ancient originals. Bronze

150
The Cameron Gallery. Bust: *Genius*. 1795
St Petersburg. Cast by EDMONDE GASTECLOUX;
copy of the original by ANTONIO CANOVA. Bronze
(commissioned by Catherine the Great)

151
The Catherine Park
The Agate Rooms (Cold Baths)
Architect: CHARLES CAMERON, 1780–88

154
The Catherine Park
The Marble (Siberian or Palladian) Bridge
Architect: VASILY NEYELOV, 1770–76

155
The Catherine Park. The Turkish Bath
Architect: HIPPOLYTO MONIGHETTI, 1829

156 >
The Catherine Park
Fountain: *Girl with a Pitcher.* 1810–17
Sculptor: PAVEL SOKOLOV; engineer:
AUGUSTINE DE BÉTHANCOURT (1996; bronze
copy from the original by PAVEL SOKOLOV)

157
The Catherine Park. The granite terrace
Statues: *Apoxyomenos* and *Venus of Medici*
1850s. Copies from ancient originals
(executed by I. GAMBURGER by the method
of galvanoplasty)

158
The Catherine Park. The granite terrace
Architect: LUIGI RUSCA, 1808–10

159 >>
The Catherine Park. The Grotto Pavilion
Architects: BARTOLOMEO FRANCESCO RASTRELLI,
ANTONIO RINALDI, 1753–57

160
The Catherine Palace. Panoramic view
of the façade from Parade Square

161
The Catherine Palace. The central gate
of the Parade Courtyard. 1752–56. After
a drawing by Bartolomeo Francesco Rastrelli
(produced by master craftsmen of
the Sestroretsk Arms Works)

162
The Catherine Palace. The central gate
of the Parade Courtyard. The openwork
wrought-iron railing with mounted
gilded decorations

163
The Catherine Park. The Hermitage Kitchen
Architect: Vasily Neyelov, 1775–76

164
The Catherine Park. The Chinese (Creaking)
Pavilion. Architect: Yury Velten, 1778–86

165
The Catherine Park. The humpbacked
bridge across the Fish Canal
Architect: VASILY NEYELOV, 1770s

166
The Catherine Park. The figure of Hercules
on the pylon of the Cameron Gallery
Sculptor: FIODOR GORDEYEV, 1786
After an ancient original

167
The Alexander Park. The Large Chines
Bridge. Architect: CHARLES CAMERON, 1780s

168
The Alexander Park
The Small Chinese Bridges. 1782–86
The Sestroretsk Arms Works

169 >>
The Alexander Park. The Cross Bridge
Architects: VASILY and ILYA NEYELOV, 1776–79

170 <<
The Alexander Park. The Chinese Village
Architects: CHARLES CAMERON, VASILY NEYELOV,
1782–96; VASILY STASOV, early 19th century

171
The Alexander Park. View of the Large
Caprice. Architect: VASILY NEYELOV,
engineer: IVAN GERALD, 1770–74;
Architect: GIACOMO QUARENGHI, 1780s

172
The Great Caprice. From the series *Twelve
Views of Tsarskoye Selo.* 1820. Lithograph
from a watercolour by VALERIAN LANGER

173
The Alexander Palace
Architect: Giacomo Quarenghi, 1792–96

174
The Alexander Palace. The Gate
Architect: Sylvio Danini, 1896

175
The Alexander Palace. The New or Large
Study of Emperor Nicholas II. 1903–06
Architect: Robert Melzer

176
The Alexander Palace. The Reception Room
of Emperor Nicholas II

177
The Lyceum. The Assembly (Great) Hall
Architect: VASILY STASOV, 1811

178
*View of the Garden Embankment towards
the Palace and the Lyceum.* From the series
Twelve Views of Tsarskoye Selo. 1820
Lithograph from a watercolour
by VALERIAN LANGER

179
The Lyceum. Architect: Ilya Neyelov,
1789–91; redesigned for the Lyceum
by the architect Vasily Stasov, 1811

180
Monument to Alexander Pushkin
in the Lyceum Garden. 1900
Sculptor: Robert Bach

PAVLOVSK

S ome twenty miles to the south of St Petersburg lies the celebrated park and palace ensemble of Pavlovsk, the fascinating product of a very short period of time, the late eighteenth century and the first quarter of the nineteenth.

In the early years of her reign, Catherine the Great, who was brought to the throne by a palace coup in 1762, concerned herself with holding onto power and also with the ennoblement of St Petersburg that had still not attained the grandeur of other European capitals. The Empress suffered from "construction mania" which, as she herself wrote, "is a devilish thing: the more you build, the more you want to build." In 1777 Catherine began the creation of a summer residence for her son Paul and his wife Maria Fiodorovna.

Catherine was a German princess by birth, belonging to the house of Anhalt-Zerbst. In 1745 she came to Russia and married the grandson of Peter the Great (the son of his elder surviving daughter Anna and the German Duke Charles of Holstein-Gottorp), the future Peter III. The coup in 1762 cost Peter III his throne and, soon after, his life. Catherine became the sole ruler of Russia. Her elder son Paul (Pavel Petrovich) was born in 1754 and knew from childhood about the tragic fate of his father. He barely remembered his father, but did not know his mother either as Catherine did not involve herself in his upbringing. They rarely saw each other, no more than once every few months. Paul was a sickly child, but he acquired a good grounding in the subjects necessary to a future emperor. He had a perfect command of four languages and a fair knowledge of mathematics, history, geography, shipbuilding and the art of warfare. While he feared his mother, Paul was nonetheless loyal to her. Paul's childhood and adolescence left their imprint on his character. He had no friends. He was quick-tempered and went in constant fear of his life.

In 1773 Catherine, concerned with the continuation of the line and the dynasty, married Paul off, but his bride Natalia Alexandrovna (Princess Wilhelmina of Hesse-Darmstadt) soon died in childbirth. Paul quickly married again, in September 1776. He was then twenty-two, already a mature man by eighteenth-century standards. His bride was again German, this time from Württemberg. On converting to Orthodoxy she took the name Maria Fiodorovna. She was a rosy-cheeked cheerful beauty, a head taller than her husband. She was interested in botany, loved nature and had busied herself with landscape gardening in her homeland. The young couple needed somewhere secluded to live at the start of a happy marriage and in 1777 Catherine presented her son with an extensive area of land (362 *desiatiny*) including two hamlets not far from the famous Tsarskoye Selo. The occasion for the gift was the birth of Paul's eldest son, Alexander. That event

delighted Catherine and she informed Europe of the arrival of "Monsieur Alexandre" after which many began thinking that she looked on him, rather than Paul, as the heir to the throne.

"The village of Pavlovskoye was founded and construction begun on 12 December 1777" – the entry reads in the historical chronicle of Pavlovsk. The creation of the palace, park pavilions and the park itself would, admittedly, take another fifty years to complete. At the beginning the wooden houses called Krik and Krak were already here, then came wooden palaces called Paullust ("Paul's Pleasure") and Marienthal ("Maria's Valley). Soon, though, Paul's family grew – the marriage produced four sons and six daughters – and required a large new masonry residence. Catherine entrusted the design of the palace to the then-fashionable architect Charles Cameron. At Pavlovsk the Scot managed for the first time in Russia to create a true architectural masterpiece that became a landmark in world art.

Cameron was faced with a difficult task. He erected his palace on a hill above the River Slavianka on the site of the wooden Paullust. After four years (1782–86), the three-storey central section crowned with a graceful colonnade was mainly completed, together with two low flanking semicircular galleries. The architecture of the palace was considerably influenced by the work of the sixteenth-century architect Andrea Palladio.

By 1786 Cameron had managed to finish a few rooms on the ground floor of the central section: the Ballroom, the White Dining-Room (with a splendid view of the Slavianka valley), the Old Drawing-Room and the Billiards Room. The interior decoration was initially carried out by Cameron's assistant, the artist Henri François Gabriel Viollier, and from 1786 by Vincenzo Brenna, who succeeded Cameron in the post of chief architect and went on to become Paul I's favourite architect. The decoration of the state rooms on the first floor of the central section – the Halls of War and Peace, the State Bedchamber, the Italian and Greek Halls – took place under his direction. The Italian Hall, the compositional centrepiece of the palace – has a round floor-plan and a splendid cupola with a skylight in the centre that illuminates the whole room. In the hours of darkness the hall is lit by bronze wall-lamps in the form of hunting horns and a splendid Russian-made chandelier. The Greek Hall was the setting for formal balls and receptions of various kinds. The main element in its decoration is the mighty Corinthian colonnade. Brenna emphasized that this hall was "the best of all that exist in the country".

The second period in the construction of Pavlovsk began after Paul succeeded his mother as ruler on 6 November 1796. The new Emperor now had the funds to continue work on his beloved palace. Brenna increased the size of the building by extending the galleries and wings upwards and constructing new blocks. In the wings, with the assistance of the sculptors Mikhail Kozlovsky and Ivan Martos, Brenna created a grand Throne Room, a Picture Gallery and the Passageway Cabinets. Living apartments were made beyond the Southern Drawing-Room. At the same time immense work was carried out in the park.

The third period in the construction of the palace came in the nineteenth century (1800–24) and is associated with the architects Quarenghi, Voronikhin and Rossi. Giacomo Quarenghi took part in the decoration of rooms on the ground floor: the Pilaster and New Studies and Maria Fiodorovna's Dressing-Room.

Andrei Voronikhin was a serf of the Stroganov family. From the age of 13, having mastered the art of icon-painting, he worked in monastery workshops. He was noticed by Count Alexander Stroganov and became his protégé. The Count was one of the richest and most educated men of his day, an advisor to three empresses and two emperors and among Catherine II's most loyal courtiers. At the turn of the nineteenth century Stroganov was head of the Imperial Academy of Arts. It was he who noticed his serf's exceptional talent for architecture and as early as the 1790s he began to entrust him with important work in his palace on Nevsky Prospekt. In 1800 Voronikhin was given a major commission to reconstruct the fountains of the Great Cascade at Peterhof. This abruptly increased the prominence and authority of the young architect and brought him closer to the court.

In 1803 Voronikhin began work at Pavlovsk. He was to make good the damage caused by a serious fire earlier in the year that had ruined the décor of many of the state rooms in the central section. In Maria Fiodorovna's living apartments the Tent and Lantern Studies and the Bedroom were finished to Voronikhin's designs. Finally, in 1822–24, Carlo Rossi completed the decorative work in the palace, constructing the Library above the Gonzago Gallery and partially replanning two rooms on the ground floor: the Ballroom and the Old Drawing-Room.

The owners managed to involve the celebrated furniture-maker Heinrich Gambs and his pupils in the decoration of the palace, and also Christian Meier and the artist Jakob Mettenleiter. Sumptuous patterned parquet floors were installed in the palace halls. They were made with fifty different types of timber grown in exotic African, Asian and American countries, including ebony and amaranth, palisander and rosewood, palm and sandalwood. Russia's lapidary works provided the palace with vases made of jasper and other semiprecious stones. Ancient works of art arrived from Italy: marble sculpture, busts and urns, and also terracotta found during the excavations at Pompeii.

Lighting devices – chandeliers, wall lights and lanterns – were specially created in gilded bronze and crystal for the halls in the Pavlovsk Palace. They include works by the Parisian craftsmen

Pierre Gouthière and Pierre-Philippe Thomire and magnificent pieces created by Russian craftsmen to drawings by Voronikhin and Rossi. In the late seventeenth century Johann (Ivan) Zech was considered one of the finest chandelier-makers in St Petersburg. The palace still contains many lighting devices produced in his workshop. Among them are the exquisite gilded bronze chandeliers made specially for the Picture Gallery in the 1790s.

Before even the foundation stone for the palace had been laid, its future owners, Paul and Maria Fiodorovna, were thinking about the architecture and decoration of its halls. With the aim of picking up new ideas for the finishing of their beloved Pavlovsk they set off in 1781 on a fourteen-month journey to Western Europe. The Grand Duke and Duchess visited Poland, Austria, Italy, France, the Netherlands and Germany, travelling under the names of Count and Countess Severny ("of the North"). Everywhere they were warmly received by the rulers. One of the most outstanding episodes of their journey was the visit to Paris and the triumphal reception accorded them at Versailles. The Russian admired the splendid works in the studios of artists and sculptors, and in factories producing tapestries and porcelain, glass and furniture. Count and Countess Severny not only received generous gifts from Louis XIV and Marie Antoinette, but also bought themselves items of interior decoration for very considerable sums. Trusting in their own taste, which was, it must be said, excellent, the owners of Pavlovsk bought for their future palace paintings, sets of furniture, an enormous number of clocks, tapestries and fabrics for the upholstering of furniture and walls. The furniture was purchased from the most celebrated makers: Henri Jacob in Paris and David Roentgen in Germa-

ny. The cost of the furniture they bought just in France was over 13,000 roubles, a colossal sum for the time. In every city they visited artists' studios and antique dealers' shops. At the Sèvres porcelain factory alone they bought items to the sum of 300,000 livres, while at the end of their visit to Paris Marie Antoinette presented Maria Fiodorovna with a unique toilet set, decorated with her coat of arms, worth 60,000 livres.

During their travels they never forgot for a single day their beloved estate, declaring that Pavlovsk brought them "more joy than all the beauties of Italy". The couple made active use of all they had seen and acquired during their European journey for the benefit of the palace being built at Pavlovsk. The collection of paintings included works by the finest European artists, such as Pompeo Batoni, Angelica Kauffmann, Hubert Robert and Jean-Baptiste Greuze.

Foreign travel revealed new aspects of Paul's character. Relaxed and speaking flawless French, he produced the impression of a native-born Frenchman. This, incidentally, had its effect on Catherine the Great, who before her son's journey (or, to be more precise, before the favourable reports of his behaviour while abroad) had treated him intolerantly at times. Perhaps as a result of the journey the Empress to a certain extent revised her opinion of Paul as a future occupant of the throne. This change evidently expressed itself in the events of 1783 when, to mark the birth of Paul's third child and first daughter (Alexandra), Catherine made her son a fabulous present – the Gatchina Palace.

What an irony of fate! The palace of Grigory Orlov, the "Russian Claudius", passed to the son of the man he had robbed of the throne and became Paul's favourite place for the remainder of his life. On Paul's orders many of the objects of art acquired for Pavlovsk were sent to Gatchina. There too extensive work was initiated to reconstruct the huge imperial palace, the largest in the suburbs of St Petersburg, work that occupied all Paul's time for many years.

The palace at Pavlovsk was left completely in the charge of Maria Fiodorovna who loved it dearly and lived there until her death in 1828. It became the focal element in the life of this intelligent, gifted, purposeful and energetic empress. This great woman devoted forty years to Pavlovsk and it was undoubtedly the crowning glory of her creative activities. She lived for sixty-seven years, bore and brought up ten children, lived through the tragic death of Paul I and did all she could to make the idyllic (in the spirit of Rousseau) Pavlovsk a prominent and significant feature of Russian cultural life.

Paul's lot was a hard one. He spent forty years as heir to the throne, and only four years, four months and four days as emperor. After conspirators cut short his life in the Mikhailovsky Castle in St Petersburg on 12 March 1801, Pavlovsk never again became an imperial residence.

Today visitors to the Pavlovsk palace are introduced to its extremely rich stock of treasures. Among them is a superb collection of Ancient Roman sculpture, the second most important in Russia (after the Hermitage). Many pieces were acquired by the original owners of Pavlovsk in Rome in 1782. The most interesting sculptures are *Boy with a Dead Bird*, *Resting Satyr*, *Girl with a Bird* and *Empress Faustina in the Guise of Venus* or *The Medici Venus*. Pope Pius VI presented several sculptures to the palace. Then, in 1787, Pavlovsk was enriched by the arrival of a unique group of ancient works of the second and first century B.C. purchased from the Lloyd Browne collection.

The palace can boast one of Russia's finest collections of painting and applied art. The works include those of famous artists who painted to the commission of the first owners of Pavlovsk – Hubert Robert, Joseph Vernet, Pompeo Battoni, Jean-Baptiste Greuze. There is also a wealth of canvases produced by the monumental artists Semion Shchedrin, Andrei Martynov, Jakob Mettenleiter, the Russian portraitists Fiodor Rokotov, Dmitry Levitsky and Vladimir Borovikovsky, and their Western fellows Jean Voille, Karl von Kügelchen and Johann Baptist Lampi.

A special place in the palace display is taken by fabrics – a fairly expensive element of interior decoration in the eighteenth century. They include tapestries from the *Don Quixote* series in the Tapestry Study and Maria Fiodorovna's Library. These were produced by Pierre François Cozette in 1780 at the Royal Gobelins Factory in Paris from cartoons by Charles Coypel. Two years later they were presented to Paul by Louis XIV. In all the palace halls and rooms, the windows were draped with beautiful curtains and the furniture upholstered with magnificent silks. Time, however, is very destructive to fabrics and so few authentic examples of drapery or upholstery now remain.

The palace has a remarkable collection of timepieces made by French craftsmen. These long-case, mantel-, table- and wall-clocks in some instances resemble architectural compositions of a kind. Many of them have unusual technical features that are no longer to be found in horological practice. The majority of them bear the marks of the clockmaker – Baillon, Berthoud, Robin, Laguesse.

A unique feature of the Pavlovsk palace are the items made of polished steel with gold hatching, chasing and facetting, produced in Tula by the celebrated Russian craftsmen Lialin and Samarin.

The Parisian master Henri Jacob produced sixteen sets of furniture for Pavlovsk. They were produced from designs drawn up specially for the halls of the palace in Russia. We know that other famous furniture-makers and -suppliers – Dominique Daguerre, Pierre Denizot and David Roentgen – provided works for the palace. In all more than two hundred items of furniture were produced abroad and very carefully delivered to Pavlovsk where they adorned the State Bedroom, the Greek Hall, the Halls of War and Peace, and other rooms. The pieces were resplendent with extremely fine gilded carving, silk upholstery, embroidery and decorative painting. The State Bedroom, for example, accommodated a magnificent carved suite made by Henri Jacob, painted and upholstered in Lyons silk. Notable in connection with the furniture produced within Russia is Andrei Voronikhin who designed sets

for the Greek Hall, Paul I's Library, the Boudoir, the Pilaster Study and the Lantern Study. His example was followed by Carlo Rossi who designed splendid furniture for the palace library (which was sadly lost during the war). It was created in Karelian birch by master craftsmen Heinrich Gambs and Vasily Bobkov.

Pavlovsk is home to one of Russia's most significant collections of Russian and Western European ceramics. There are large gala dining services and sets designed for two people, sumptuous vases for the decoration of the halls and porcelain insets for furniture. The Western European porcelain was produced at the Sèvres factory in France, the Meissen, Berlin and Ludwigsburg factories in Germany. English pottery came from the Chelsea and Derby factories, from the workshops of Spode and Wedgwood. Russian porcelain was produced at the Imperial Porcelain Factory in St Petersburg. Among those involved in its creation were the sculptors Stepan Pimenov and Alexei Voronikhin (the architect's nephew), the painters Golov, Meshcheriakov and Kannunikov. Porcelain articles adorn almost all the halls in the palace. In Maria Fiodorovna's dressing-room on the ground floor visitors' attention is taken by the 34-piece Green Toilet Set that is decorated with gilding and grisaille painting. All the ceramics came into the palace during Maria Fiodorovna's lifetime and were carefully preserved as precious heirlooms by the subsequent owners.

The Pavlovsk park extends on both sides of the little unhurriedly flowing River Slavianka. The park was created in the English landscape style in which nature seems to surround the human being and everything is simple and natural in the spirit of the philosophers Jean-Jacques Rousseau and Montaigne who asserted that a man's highest morality comes from his affinity to nature.

The park, one of the largest in Russia, was formed at the turn of the nineteenth century when the English way of making parks in imitation of a natural landscape was becoming fashionable in Europe and Russia. The Pavlovsk park is embellished by a variety of architectural monuments, notable among which is the Temple of Friendship designed by Charles Cameron.

At the entrance to the park Cameron constructed the Apollo Colonnade which he conceived as a sanctuary of poetry, the realm of the muses and their leader, the god of the arts Apollo.

The Dairy and Aviary were erected in complete accordance with ideas Maria Fiodorovna had cherished even before her marriage. Cameron built the Dairy in 1782 in the style of a Swiss rural house. The walls were faced with granite boulders and the roof thatched with straw. Such buildings served as a reminder of country pastimes, closeness to nature and cosy family life. With time, thirty-seven pavilions, obelisks and "ruins" appeared in the park. They were created in different styles, but are all tasteful and refined. Notable among them are the Peel Tower, the Cold Bathhouse (for bathing in summer), the Green Labyrinth, the Open-Air Theatre and Amphitheatre, as well as the Old Silvia area with its statues of Apollo, Flora, Callipygian Venus, Mercury and the nine Muses and Paul's Mausoleum.

The park occupied low hills surrounded by ponds, weirs and waterfalls. The owners of Pavlovsk took care to ensure that the park was kept replenished with fruit trees from Moscow, oaks from southern Finland and limes from the German city of Lübeck. Devoted care and attention made it possible to create a rose garden in which no fewer than a thousand plants bloomed. The Private Garden located beneath the windows of Maria Fiodorovna's apartments required several thousand pots of flowers each year.

Pavlovsk gradually developed into an encyclopaedia of landscape architecture. Its different localities reflected the main traditions in the laying out of European gardens in the eighteenth and nineteenth centuries – the English style predominated, but around the palace itself there was a French layout; the Private Garden was in the Dutch style, while the Great Circles area featured regular parterres adorned by Classical sculpture. The Italian style was represented by the Stone Steps with cast-iron lions at their base and a pair of marble lions at the top. The Pavlovsk park was the setting for tremendous festivities, much of the organization of which was the work of the artist Pietro Gonzago who was also a celebrated landscape gardener. He was of the opinion that "the skill of the gardener lies in the fact that, having sensed the character of the objects around him that nature has scattered in a disorderly manner, he subordinates them to a particular order so as to enhance the effect of those objects on a person." It took years of work for Gonzago to achieve what he had imagined. He turned impenetrable thickets into a park that was shaped by a single conception with groves of trees linked by paths and alleys leading to meadows, ponds and the Slavianka.

For Maria Fiodorovna the beautiful park was the place in which her talent and artistic taste were concentrated. After Paul's death, the Dowager Empress changed the pattern of social life at Pavlovsk that had become established in the Emperor's last years. It became the venue for musical evenings and theatrical gatherings. A play specially written for Pavlovsk by the poet Gavriil Derzhavin was performed in the palace. A circle of men of letters formed around Maria Fiodorovna and she was on friendly terms with them. It included the prominent poet Vasily Zhukovsky, the fable-writer Ivan Krylov and Nikolai Karamzin, the first Russian historian of Russia.

Vue des environs du Château de Pavlowsky.

< The Pavlovsk Park. The Memorial to the Parents Pavilion
Architect: CHARLES CAMERON, 1787; sculptor: IVAN MARTOS, 1803
(the sculpture installed in 1807). Marble

View of the Environs of the Pavlovsk Palace. 1821–22
Lithograph tinted in watercolour. By ANDREI MARTYNOV

The Rose Pavilion in the Pavlovsk Park. Early 19th century
Watercolour by an unknown artist

The traditions of cultural development associated with Pavlovsk though the gatherings here of artists, composers, poets and performers, became established in the time of the first owners of the palace and were continued after Maria Fiodorovna's death. Music held a special place – it was at Pavlovsk that the Russian composer and pianist Dmitry Bortniansky first demonstrated his talents. That marked the start of the palace's brilliant and varied musical life. In 1838 Russia's first railway line was constructed between St Petersburg and Pavlovsk. The terminus was located in the park, not far from the palace. The board of the railway decided to organize concerts in Pavlovsk and engaged the leading conductors and performers of the day. The music of the celebrated Russian composer Mikhail Glinka was played in the station building, but Pavlovsk reached the height of its popularity when the composer and conductor Johann Strauss – the Waltz King, as he was known in the nineteenth century – gave concerts here.

The Rose Pavilion is one of the most romantic sights of Pavlovsk. It stands on a picturesque spot at the meeting-point of three areas in the huge park: the Old Woods (or Old Sylvia), the White Birch and the Parade Ground with its smooth ponds. Superb views of the pavilion can be had from those ponds.

At the end of the eighteenth century, the Parade Ground was a dusty, open expanse of sand used, as the name suggests, for military parades. Alongside lay the extensive grounds of General Piotr Bagration's dacha that Dowager Empress purchased in the summer of 1811. Maria Fiodorovna entrusted the reconstruction of the dacha to Andrei Voronikhin. The architect constructed a light, elegant wooden structure that is an unique, unique of its kind, of early-nineteenth-century Russian Classical architecture. To the architect's design garden paths were laid out around the pavilion and between them beds planted with sweet-smelling roses which gave the building its name. Beneath the pediment on the main façade an inscription was added in gilded bronze letters, the French words "PAVILLON DES ROSES". Flowers and depictions of them adorned its interiors, but the real kingdom of flowers was outside the building. The new pavilion became a favourite place for the Empress to spend hot summer days and warm quiet evenings.

Right up until the Empress's death in 1828, the Rose Pavilion played a significant role in Russian culture. Poets and prose writers, such as Vasily Zhukovsky, Yury Neledinsky-Meletsky, Nikolai Karamzin, Ivan Krylov and Nikolai Gnedich presented their latest works here, while others who attended the literary gatherings included Konstantin Batiushkov, Ivan Dmitriyev, Alexei Olenin and Alexander Turgenev.

The history of the Pavlovsk palace and park reflects the story of many generations. Pavlovsk was reborn after the Second World War as an architectural ensemble and museum through the immense efforts of the restorers and now occupies a worthy place among the "necklace" of imperial suburbs around St Petersburg.

The marriage of Paul I and Maria Fiodorovna produced the dynasty that ruled Russia down to 1917. That is not the important thing, however. We feel greater sympathy for what those people did for the country in terms of culture, morality and a benevolent attitude.

Pavlovsk is beautiful, like any child produced in love. It was born of the dreams of a woman in love, who once wrote, "The Grand Duke is the most delightful husband. My dear spouse is simply an angel and I am madly in love with him."

Here every turn of a path, every corner in the palace apartments promises delight. In contrast to brilliant Peterhof, the gleaming Catherine Palace at Tsarskoye Selo and mysterious Gatchina, Pavlovsk was created for living in and not for show. All its quirks – the dairies, chalets and huts – are not merely tributes to fashion that had, of course, moved on since the older imperial residences were built; they are also reflections of a desire to shelter a beloved spouse from the tragic, intrigue-filled life of the court.

181 <<
Pavlovsk. The Central Block
of the Great Palace and the side colonnades
Architects: CHARLES CAMERON, 1782–86;
VINCENZO BRENNA, 1797–99

182
The Pavlovsk Palace. The Upper Vestibule
Architect: VINZENZO BRENNA, 1789

183
G. SCHWARZ
*Sentry Mounting in the Upper Vestibule
during the Reign of Paul I.* 1848
Oil on canvas

184 >>
The Pavlovsk Palace
The Egyptian or Lower Vestibule
Architect: CHARLES CAMERON, 1786

188
The Pavlovsk Palace. The Carpet Study
Architect: ANDREI VORONIKHIN,
1803–04

189
The Pavlovsk Palace
Fireplace decoration: *Reader*
Late 18th century. After a model
by L. BOIZOT. France
Gilded and patinated bronze

190
The Pavlovsk Palace. The Carpet Study
Desk of Paul I. 1800. After a drawing
by VINCENZO BRENNA. St Petersburg
Mahogany decorated with ivory,
gilded bronze and milk glass

191
The Pavlovsk Palace. The Hall of War
Architects: VINCENZO BRENNA, 1789;
ANDREI VORONIKHIN, 1803–04

192
The Pavlovsk Palace. The Greek Hall. Detail

193 >>
The Pavlovsk Palace. View of the Hall
of War from the Greek Hall

194
The Pavlovsk Palace. The Greek Hall
Architects: Vincenzo Brenna, 1780s;
Andrei Voronikhin, 1803–04

195
The Pavlovsk Palace
The Large Throne Room
Architect: Vincenzo Brenna, 1797–99

196
The Pavlovsk Palace. The Large Throne
Room. Girandole. Late 18th century
The Imperial Glassworks, St Petersburg
The Paris Service. 1780s
The Sèvres royal factory. Porcelain

197
The Pavlovsk Palace. The Library
of Maria Fiodorovna. Detail

198
Johann Gottlieb Pullmann
Portrait of Grand Duchess Maria Fiodorovna
1782–83. Copy from a portret by Pompeo
Girolamo Batoni. Oil on canvas

199 >>
The Pavlovsk Palace
The Library of Maria Fiodorovna
Architects: Vincenzo Brenna, 1792;
Andrei Voronikhin, 1803–04

201
The Pavlovsk Palace. The State Bedroom
Couch. 1784. The Henri Jacob Workshop,
Paris; designed by Dugoure (?); upholstery
after a design by V. VAN LEHEN; painted
decoration by JACOB METTENLEITER,
St Petersburg. Carved and gilded wood

202
The Pavlovsk Palace. Clock featuring
a scene from the opera *Le Déserteur*
by Pierre Alexandre Monsigny. 1770s. France
Gilded bronze; box with musical mechanism Late 18th century. Russia. Karelian
birch wood and gilded bronze

200 <<
The Pavlovsk Palace. The State Bedroom
Architect: VINCENZO BRENNA, 1792

203 <
The Pavlovsk Palace
The Room of Cavaliers-in-Attendance
Architect: Vincenzo Brenna, 1797–99

204
The Pavlovsk Palace. The Picture Gallery
Architect: Vincenzo Brenna, 1798

208
The Pavlovsk Palace. The Pilaster Study
Architect: GIACOMO QUARENGHI, 1797–99

209
The Pavlovsk Palace. Calendar clock. 1790s
Clockmaster: Guidamour, Paris
Marble and gilded and patinated bronze

210
The Pavlovsk Palace. The Lantern Study
Architect: ANDREI VORONIKHIN, 1807

211
The Pavlovsk Palace. Cup depicting
Grand Duke Pavel Petrovich. Saucer. 1782
The Sèvres royal factory. Porcelain

212
The Pavlovsk Park. The Temple of Friendship
Architect: CHARLES CAMERON, 1780–82

213
The Pavlovsk Park. The Peel Tower
Architect: VINCENZO BRENNA, 1795;
wall decoration by PIETRO GONZAGO, 1797

214 >>
The Pavlovsk Park. View of the Great Palace
from the River Slavianka

215
The Pavlovsk Park. The Temple of Friendship
Architect: Charles Cameron, 1780–82

216
The Pavlovsk Palace
View of the valley of the River Slavianka
from the Large Stone (Italian) Staircase
Architect: Vincenzo Brenna, 1799. Lion
18th century. Italy. Marble

217 >>
The Pavlovsk Park
View of the Apollo Colonnade
Architect: Charles Cameron, 1782–1783

218
The Pavlovsk Park. The Visconti Bridge
Architects: Vincenzo Brenna
and Placido Visconti, 1803

219 >
The Pavlovsk Park. View from the Bridge
over the Ruin Cascade to the Peel Tower

220 >
The Pavlovsk Park. Bridge over the Ruin
Cascade. Architect: Vincenzo Brenna, 1793–94

221
The Pavlovsk Park. The Old Sylvia. *Apollo Belvedere.* 1782. Russia
Cast by EDMONDE GASTECLOUX; wax model by FIODOR GORDEYEV
Copy from an ancient original. Bronze

222
The Pavlovsk Park. The Old Sylvia. *Venus Callipygos.* 1780. Russia
Cast by EDMONDE GASTECLOUX; wax model by FIODOR GORDEYEV
Copy from an ancient original. Bronze

223
The Pavlovsk Park. The Old Sylvia. *Calliope,* the muse of epic poetry
and eloquence. 1792. Russia. Cast by EDMONDE GASTECLOUX; wax model
by FIODOR GORDEYEV. Copy from an ancient original. Bronze

224 >>
The Pavlovsk Park. The Old Sylvia. *Urania,* the muse
of astronomy. 1780. Russia. Cast by EDMONDE GASTECLOUX; wax model
by FIODOR GORDEYEV. Copy from an ancient original. Bronze

225
The Pavlovsk Park. The Dairy
Architect: Charles Cameron, 1782

226
The Pavlovsk Park. The Round Hall
Architects: Giacomo Quarenghi,
Vincenzo Brenna, 1799–1800

227 >>
The Pavlovsk Park
View of the River Slavianka
and the Centaur Bridge

228
The Pavlovsk Park. Bridge near
the Northern Block of the Great Palace
Architect: Vincenzo Brenna, 1799

229
The Pavlovsk Park. The Cast-Iron Bridge
near the Temple of Friendship. 1823
The Clark Iron Foundry

230
The Pavlovsk Park. The Centaur Bridge
Architect: Charles Cameron, 1799

231
The Pavlovsk Park
The Pavilion of the Three Graces
Architect: Charles Cameron, 1800–01;
sculptors: Paolo Triscorni,
Ivan Prokofyev (bas-relief)

232 >>
The Pavlovsk Park. View of the Great
Palace and the Centaur Bridge

Vue
du
Palais
Oranienbaum
1758

ORANIENBAUM

The absolute authenticity that provides a special flavour and atmosphere of the past makes Oranienbaum unique, setting it apart from the other imperial residences forming the brilliant "necklace" around the south of St Petersburg. "A true wonder, full of eighteenth-century wonders" is how the famous Russian art-historian and artist Igor Grabar described Oranienbaum.

The palace-and-park ensemble at Oranienbaum began to form in the time of Peter the Great. Created as the grand residence of the Emperor's leading subject, the Illustrious Prince Alexander Menshikov, it became the physical embodiment of Russia's triumph in the Northern War against Sweden. From here Menshikov directed work on the fortifications and naval stronghold of Kronstadt.

The Great (Menshikov) Palace was built in the Baroque style by Giovanni Fontana and Johann Gottfried Schädel with the assistance of Andreas Schlüter. Despite repeated later reconstructions, it has retained its original exterior appearance.

The Izhora heights extending along the south shore of the Gulf of Finland were an ideal place for the construction of the Oranienbaum, Peterhof and Strelna palaces. Those residences and the chain of estates belonging to the great figures of Peter's reign that lay between them formed a magnificent panorama to delight the eyes of all who arrived in the new Russian capital by sea.

The construction of Menshikov's palace began no later than 1710, while the date when the palace church was consecrated, 3 September 1727, can be considered that of its completion (the more so since five days later the "Illustrious Prince" was arrested prior to his banishment). By that time the appearance of the palace had been established and the ensemble of gardens and adjoining ancillary structures formed. The palace had two grand façades: the southern façade overlooks the Upper Park, the other, northern façade is a broad 210-metre-long arc facing the sea – a "crescent moon" as the French diplomat Aubry de LaMottraye described it. The compositional centre of the edifice is a two-storey block with a tall mansard roof rising to a belvedere lantern that is topped by a princely crown. It was adjoined by sweeping single-storey side galleries that ended in twin domed pavilions 26 metres high. The western pavilion contained the palace church and the eastern pavilion had the Japanese Hall.

For all its scale and outward grandeur, the palace was cosy and elegant inside. It contained 76 relatively small rooms. Two were set aside for the personal use of Peter the Great and the Tsar made use of the palace's celebrated Turkish bath to improve his health. The second storey contained the ceremonial apartments and was occupied by the owners. The noble Holsteiner Friedrich Wilhelm von Bergholtz reported that "the rooms in the palace are small, but decorated with splen-

did paintings and furniture." The interior appearance was splendidly enhanced by decorative paintings produced under the direction of Ivan Vishniakov, tiles, marbles, fabrics and tooled leather on the walls, patterned parquet floors and Ivan Zarudny's gilded and silvered sculpture in the iconostasis of the palace church. Work on the church began in the summer of 1719. Its consecration to the martyred physician St Panteleimon was no coincidence: the Russian naval victories at Hangö and Grönhamn took place on his feast-day.

Peter enjoyed visiting his bosom companion at Oranienbaum, a fact borne out by the court journals from 1713 onwards. A characteristic feature of Peter's time that can still be observed in several places was the creation of large central state rooms in residences that were used for important ceremonies, receptions, gala dinners, theatrical performances, spectacles and balls. These include the Great (or White) Hall in the Menshikov Palace. On important occasions abundant feasts were given here

with up to two hundred dishes served on precious tableware. The festivities became especially frequent during the reign of the young Emperor Peter II in the summer of 1727. Menshikov amused the teenage monarch with rich hunting and chasing as the woods around Oranienbaum abounded in wildfowl and game, including even the rare blue fox.

After the fall of the "excessively proud Goliath" (as contemporaries described Menshikov), the palace passed to the state for use as a naval hospital, but it managed to avoid any radical reconstruction.. Following the arrival in Russia of the future Peter III, Oranienbaum was adapted for use as an imperial residence. The construction work was supervised by Bartolomeo Francesco Rastrelli. The architect first came to Oranienbaum

"to view the works" on 28 September 1748. Later, as he himself stated, "the Grand Duke commissioned me to remake his suburban palace in the present-day style... This building was completed in the course of two years. The brilliant master of grand, opulent richly elaborate Baroque architecture, approached the conversion of the palace for use as a grand-ducal residence with rare delicacy. While leaving the exterior decoration of the palace as it was for the most part, he devoted great efforts to the design of the southern façade. An extensive service wing was added to the eastern, Japanese, pavilion, mirroring the existing one on the western side. Diverging slightly, these wings formed a grand courtyard – a *court d'honneur* – that was a favourite feature in Rastrelli's designs for suburban residences.

The Japanese Pavilion, like the palace as a whole, was repeatedly reconstructed. In the 1730s it was intended to accommodate the anatomical theatre attached to the Naval Hospital. In 1748–53 the building was converted into a "hermitage" – the name then given to a dining-room with a table that could be raised and lowered to ensure the privacy of the diners. In 1761 a new style interior for the pavilion was commissioned. The walls were adorned with stucco mouldings and little shelves on elaborate consoles for the display of Japanese and Chinese porcelain. The pavilion acquired its oriental name. In the following century the building was again repeatedly redecorated and refurbished.

On 29 June 1762 the palace was the setting for an important historical event: on his own name-day Peter III signed the declaration of his "voluntary and unforced" abdication. He would never return to Oranienbaum. His wife, the new ruler, also left the residence. Only four years after taking the throne did Catherine the Great return and issue a host of instructions for its improvement. The work at Oranienbaum was carried out under the direction of an architect representing the new, Classical, trend – Antonio Rinaldi. In 1772–75 he reconstructed the terraces and steps that give the palace's northern façade its picturesque grandeur.

The Great Palace ensemble includes the Lower Garden, one of the first regular gardens in Russia. On the edge of the Lower Garden, by the road to Koporye, stands the building called the Picture House which dates back to the first quarter of the eighteenth century. In Grand Duke Peter's time it was the venue for shows and concerts. Special rooms were set aside for the Library and Cabinet of Curioisities, as well as for the Picture Gallery.

In the eastern area of the Upper Park, on the high bank of the little River Karost, stand the buildings of the Peterstadt ensemble – the Palace of Peter III and the Gate of Honour. At one time two fortresses stood here, to the south of the Great Palace, successors to the "toy" fortresses with which Peter the Great amused himself in his youth. One of them, which appeared in 1746, was

house, an arsenal, premises for the court official responsible for hot drinks, a house for the chamberlain and other buildings. Today only the entrance gate that led to the arsenal yard has survived. This Gate of Honour is topped by a turret and a weathervane that shows the date of its construction – 1757. The Peterstadt gate is an extremely rare and unparalleled example of small-scale architecture from the mid-eighteenth century.

The creative success of the Italian architect Antonio Rinaldi, who arrived in Russia in 1752, effectively began with Oranienbaum, although he was by that time already a mature master. "Under the supervision of the architect Rinaldi … a masonry house has been made in the fortress under construction." This document refers to the creation of what we call the Palace of Peter III, begun in 1758. The interior decoration was completed in 1762, the year that proved fateful for its owner.

The two-storey brick building is not very large. It has a square ground plan with one corner where the entrance was located cut away. Above the entrance is an elegant balcony with a grille. Niches flanking the entrance contain marble busts. A wooden balustrade runs along the edge of the roof.

The ground floor is in the nature of service premises. A spiral staircase with granite steps leads to the upper storey. There are six rooms on this floor: the Anteroom, Buffet Room, Picture Hall, Study, Bedroom and Boudoir. The palace rooms have in part retained their original finish. The elements employed in the decoration are very varied: moulding, carving, easel painting and lacquer murals, fabrics and patterned parquet flooring. The miniature Buffet Room has kept its unusually finished walls. Twenty-two little console shelves serving as the bases for porcelain articles form a single composition with the Chinese statuettes and vases. Rinaldi reused this idea with even greater effect in the Coasting Hill Pavilion.

The Picture Hall is the largest room in the palace and also served as a state reception and dining room. Its original appearance underwent considerable change in the nineteenth century. In 1961–62 the main features were recreated, above all the paintings that adorned it. We know that in 1762, in keeping with Rinaldi's project, the academician Jakob von Stählin and the painter Conrad Pfandzelt installed Peter III's rich collection of paintings here following the "tapestry" principle. The walls were lined with a solid covering of 63 canvases by Italian, Dutch, German and Flemish artists of the seventeenth century and the first half of the eighteenth. The marvellous lacquer decorative painting "in the Chinese style" has come down to us in its original form. We know that "in February 1762 Fiodor Vlasov decorated with lacquer work the doors, panels and frames of the palace." In all there are 218 separate lacquer paintings here.

Not far from Peterstadt is the Lower Pond. In Grand Duke Peter's time it was termed "the Amusement Sea" and was the scene of naval battles involving a 20-gun ship, a frigate and two galleys.

The name "Russian Switzerland" became attached to the area of the park around the palace which was redesigned in the nineteenth century. It is marked by a special romantic atmosphere enhanced by a host of bridges, ruins and waterfalls. This remarkable example of a landscape park was created by the master-gardener Joseph Bush in the 1830s.

While she was still Grand Duchess, Catherine the Great contemplated the creation of a small private residence at Oranienbaum. She only managed to realize her idea in full measure, however, after she became Empress. That is how the Private Dacha

named Yekaterinburg in honour of St Catherine, the saint whose name was adopted by the Grand Duke's young bride. Ten years later the beginnings of a whole garrison town were laid. These military "objects" were created for Charles Peter Ulrich of Holstein-Gottorp who came to Russia from Kiel in February 1742, took the name and title of Grand Duke Peter Fiodorovich and was proclaimed heir to the Russian throne. The childless Empress Elizabeth was arranging for the future of the dynasty and her nephew and appointed Oranienbaum to be his summer residence.

Not only the life-story of the future Emperor, but even his very appearance in the world was exceptional: the son of Grand Duchess Anna Petrovna and Duke Charles Frederick of Schleswig-Holstein was grandson to Peter the Great and great nephew of Charles XII of Sweden. Such was the complicated pedigree of the future Russian monarch who was born in Kiel in 1728. He might have occupied the Swedish throne, but fate decided otherwise.

It should be noted to the credit of the newly-designated heir that within a year of his arrival in Russia he had mastered the basics of the Russian language and "had a firm knowledge of the main features of Russian history." His true delight, however, was "to see soldiers trooping during a parade." The French diplomat Jean-Louis Favier recalled: "He has the appearance of a complete military man. He is permanently got up in a uniform of such tight and short cut following the Prussian fashion…" Peter's aunt, the Empress, gave him permission in 1755 to send for a platoon of soldiers from Holstein. The fortress named in honour of St Peter that was erected for them was fitted out like a true military stronghold.

Work carried out over a period of less than ten years turned a small fortress with five bastions into a more imposing citadel of greater complexity. The complex included a commandant's

Unknown 18th-century artist
Portrait of Grand Duke Piotr Fiodorovich
Oil on canvas

VIGILIUS ERICHSEN
*Portrait of Catherine the Great
before a Mirror.* After 1762. Oil on canvas

appeared. Recalling the year 1757, Catherine later wrote: "I busied myself then at Oranienbaum with the laying out of what is known there as my garden, and planting things in it."

The "Private Dacha" is made up of the Chinese Palace (1762–68) and the Coasting Hill Pavilion (1762–74), both by Rinaldi, as well as the Upper Park around those two buildings.

The summer amusement palace was called "Chinese" on account of the opulent decoration of four rooms in keeping with contemporary conceptions of the art of China and the Orient in general. While remaining an entirely European edifice, it testifies to the aesthetic passions of its crowned owner and the fashion of the time. Naturally works by Oriental artists and craftsmen played a leading role in its artistic decoration.

"The Chinese Palace is a pearl unique of its sort, a work of art with such integrity, such harmony, such superb execution – such a grand, exquisite knick-knack that, looking at it, one simply has to fall in love. The painted patterns, the stucco ornament, the paintings, the architectural details – all of these are linked in a single inseparable whole that has in its purely musical effect something in common with the sonatas of Haydn and Mozart," wrote Alexander Benois. Modest on the outside, the palace has interiors that are simply stunning. The succession of rooms that follow each other seemingly competing in terms of refinement and fanciful inventiveness present every possible variation of the stylistic devices of the Rococo. The exquisiteness of the interiors is underlined by the use of stylized Oriental motifs and the incorporation of genuine works of art from China and Japan.

The Buglework Cabinet, the Damask Bedchamber, the Hall of the Muses, the Blue and Pink Drawing-Rooms, the Stucco Room...

The very names suggest the exceptional outstanding nature of the palace interiors. A tour around these halls will not disappoint the highest expectations. Rinaldi has used all the rich arsenal of decorative forms that characterized the Rococo, achieving a unity between the architecture of the palace and its decoration. There is delicate moulding with a variety of patterns, rich woodcarving, painted ceilings and unique parquet floors. Those floors, produced to Rinaldi's designs, are unequalled in Russian decorative art and cover an area of 722 square metres. They are made up of a wide range of different timbers – oak, maple, birch, rosewood, box, mahogany, ebony, Persian walnut, amaranth – and are striking for the complexity and originality of the pattern, technical virtuosity and inspired execution. The floors were assembled by skilled Russian woodworkers under the direction of gifted foreign craftsmen then working in Russia. Plant ornament in which flowers, branches, wreathes and leaves are elaborately intertwined form a composition that never repeats itself in shape or in colour scheme.

No less interesting is the decorative painting in the Chinese Palace. Every hall is adorned by a ceiling painting. Thirteen of them were produced by artists belonging to the Venetian Academy of Arts – Gaspare Diziani, Giovanni Battista Pittoni, Francesco Zugno, Domenico Maggiotto and Jacopo Guarana – to a special commission, while the celebrated artists Stefano Torelli and Serafino Barozzi created their ceiling paintings directly in the palace. Mythological characters act out uncomplicated scenes with exquisite grace against a background of sky and clouds within fanciful moulded frames. Ornamental murals and painted panels also adorn the walls of the halls.

The decoration of the walls in the Buglework Cabinet is unique. Under the supervision of the Frenchwoman Marie de Chelles, in a year and a half nine Russian needlewomen embroidered twelve panels in different coloured silk and chenille. The background for the work was made of mother-of-pearl bugles (elongated glass beads) that set off the gentle colours of the silks to great effect. The Buglework Cabinet is an exceptional phenomenon in decorative and applied art: there is nothing else like it. Mosaic furniture made with coloured smalts produced by the Russian polymath Mikhailo Lomonosov – again unique of its kind – is on display in the Buglework Cabinet.

Rare examples of bugle and chenille work on straw can be seen in the Damask Bedchamber. In the Large Chinese Cabinet the walls are decorated with marquetry panels with subjects of an oriental nature. They are matched by the furniture: low Japanese black lacquer cupboards with chased fittings and decorative painting; red and black lacquer boxes; and eighteenth-century Chinese chairs. A collection of seventeenth- and eighteenth-century Chinese

The Coasting Hill Pavilion at Oranienbaum. 1895
Watercolour by Alexander Benois

Portrait of Grand Duchess Yelena Pavlovna. 1830s
Lithograph by an unknown artist

porcelain painted with cobalt completes the decoration of the cabinet. In keeping with mid-eighteenth-century tastes, the interiors of all the halls in the palace were adorned by Western European as well as Oriental porcelain. The Meissen collection includes a wide variety of objects, pride of place among which is taken by sculptural groups by Johann Joachim Kändler and Michel Victor Acier.

The Chinese Palace with its unique interiors and décor reflect the Russian interpretation of the Rococo style. According to Alexander Benois, "The astonishingly beautiful and balanced ensemble of the Chinese Palace should hold one of the foremost places in the history of eighteenth-century art."

The northern façade of the palace has retained its original appearance. Its southern counterpart was given a new look by Ludwig Bohnstedt and Andrei Stakenschneider in the middle of the nineteenth century when it became two-storeyed.

Still today the Coasting Hill Pavilion occupies an exceptional place in the Private Dacha ensemble. The pavilion rises above the natural coastal terrace in the form of a three-storey building crowned by a dome and was once the main architectural element in a very elaborate piece of engineering. The prototype for the imperial Coasting Hill was the icy slopes descending which was one of the commonest winter amusements in Russia. The tracks constructed at Oranienbaum in 1762–68 were undoubtedly the greatest created for use in summer. The complex included

the slopes themselves, the pavilion and a covered, colonnaded gallery. The descent began from the third storey of the pavilion. The carts sat one or two people. They were "gilded and decorated with rich carving [and] took the form of ancient chariots, gondolas, saddled lions, bears…" The sloping track adjoining the pavilion ran for 532 metres, while the roof of the gallery could be used as a place to stroll. Catherine II herself went down the track with her beloved grandson, the future Emperor Alexander I. It was this very pavilion that "many a time accommodated our sovereign Catherine the Great with all her brilliant court and after the summer coasting she simply treated all the courtiers to tea."

Today the pavilion is all that remains of the complex that as early as Paul I's reign was declared dilapidated and "in danger of collapse" and closed on the Emperor's orders. The interior decoration is magnificent in this building whose rooms are filled with light and air. Murals, moulding and gilding adorn its walls, vaults and ceilings. The only artificial marble floor in Russia has survived here.

The true gem of the pavilion is the Porcelain Cabinet. It was intended for a set of porcelain ornaments produced in Meissen

to Catherine II's special commission in 1772–75. The set glorified in allegorical form the great Russian naval victory at Chesme in 1770 that was a decisive moment in the Russo-Turkish War.

Close by the Coasting Hill Pavilion is the "Stone Hall" built to Rastrelli's plans by M. G. Hofmann. Today, as in the past, this building is used for theatrical performances and concerts.

In 1827 Emperor Nicholas I granted Oranienbaum to his brothers. The once brilliant "paradise" became a grand-ducal and later a ducal country estate. For many years it belonged to Grand Duke Mikhail Pavlovich and his wife, Yelena Pavlovna, the daughter of a prince of Württemberg who took special pains to improve the estate. Yelena Pavlovna enjoyed fine taste, a broad education and a variety of interests and pursuits. She initiated the formation of the Russian Music Society and assisted in the creation of the St Petersburg Conservatory. The first rector of the latter, the composer Anton Rubinstein, was a frequent guest at Oranienbaum. Yelena Pavlovna was mistress here for almost half a century, and for half that long period (1849–73) the sole owner of the estate. The architects Andrei Stakenschneider, Harald Bosse and Ludwig Bohnstedt were invited to work at Oranienbaum. The last was responsible for the conversion of the Maid-of-Honour's Pavilion near the Chinese Palace into the Chinese Kitchen.

In 1839 the noted French traveller and writer Astolphe de Custine wrote: "With her inherent taste Grand Duchess Yelena has turned Oranienbaum into a delightful spot in defiance of the doleful locality and memories of the tragedy that took place here... Terraces, steps and gentle slopes drowning in flowers connect the palace with the park and adorn it exceedingly."

After Yelena Pavlovna's death, Oranienbaum passed to her daughter Yekaterina Mikhailovna, the wife of Duke George of Mecklenburg-Strelitz. Their children – George, Michael and Helena (who married the Prince of Saxe-Altenburg in 1891) – were to be the last owners of the residence before its nationalization. Duke George (the Younger) and his daughter Natalia (Karlova) found their last resting place in the Oranienbaum park. The year 1917, an epoch for all of Russia, also changed the life of Oranienbaum and its owners.

In the summer of 1922 a museum opened in the Chinese Palace, the gem of the ensemble. Work on its creation had begun immediately after the nationalization of the palatial residence in

The Lower Gardens and the Church Block of the Great Palace at Oranienbaum. 1901
Watercolour by Alexander Benois

Karl Briullov
Grand Duchess Yekaterina Mikhailovna. 1845
Oil on canvas

1918. Among those involved in the establishment of the museum were such prominent cultural figures as Alexander Benois, S. K. Isakov and Vladimir Levinson-Lessing.

The fate of the museum and its collections has been difficult and at times dramatic. Losses have befallen it on several occasions. During the Second World War, fortunately, the small Oranienbaum pocket held out and the enemy did not enter the estate. The damage inflicted by the war did not ruin the appearance of its edifices and the skilled mastery of the restorers has only further brought out their superb artistic qualities. That brilliant product of the Rococo era, the Chinese Palace, has been acknowledged as a cultural monument of world significance. Like the Coasting Hill Pavilion and the Palace of Peter III it has for the most part retained its mid-eighteenth-century decoration. These are the only architectural monuments in the imperial residences around St Petersburg to have come down to us in an authentic state. In the 1950s museums opened in the Palace of Peter III and the Coasting Hill Pavilion. Efforts to turn Menshikov's Great Palace into a museum began in the 1990s, but still today two-thirds of the building does not belong to the museum.

At present the Oranienbaum Museum Reserve consists of three ensembles – the Great Palace with the Lower Park, Peterstadt and the Private Dacha.

233 <
Oranienbaum. The Great (Menshikov)
Palace. The main block. 1710–1722
Architects: Giovanni Fontana,
Johann Gottfried Schädel

234
The Great (Menshikov) Palace
The Japanese Pavilion
Interior of the Japanese Hall

235
Friedrich Barisien
*The Great Palace. View from the Lower
Pond.* 1758. Oil on canvas

236 >>
The Great (Menshikov) Palace
View of the Japanese Pavilion from
the Lower Pond. Architects: Jean-Baptiste
Le Blond, Nicholas Pineau (?), 1719

237
Oranienbaum. Peterstadt. The Palace
of Peter III. 1759–62. The Entrance
(Honourary) Gate. Architect:
ANTONIO RINALDI, 1757

238
The Stone Hall
Architects: BARTOLOMEO FRANCESCO RASTRELLI,
M. G. HOFMANN (?), 1750–52

239
Peterstadt. The Palace of Peter III

240
Peterstadt. The Palace of Peter III
The Picture Room

241
Peterstadt. The Palace of Peter III
The Picture Room. Lacquer panel. 1762
By Fiodor Vlasov

242
Peterstadt
The Palace of Peter III. The Picture Room
Unknown 18th-century painter. Germany
Old Money-Changer Weighing Coins
Oil on canvas

243
Peterstadt
The Palace of Peter III. The Picture Room
JAN PAUWEL GILLEMANS. *Still Life with a Black Man*. Oil on canvas

244
Peterstadt. The Palace of Peter III
The Study

245
Peterstadt. The Palace of Peter III
The Study. Detail

246
Peterstadt. The Palace of Peter III
The Buffet Room

247
Peterstadt. The Palace of Peter III
The Bedroom

248
Peterstadt. The Palace of Peter III
The Bedroom. Bureau. 1759
By FRANCISK CONRAD. Painted wood

249 <
Oranienbaum
The Coasting Hill Pavilion. Eastern façade
Architect: Antonio Rinaldi, 1762–74

250
The Coasting Hill Pavilion
Eastern façade. Detail

251
The Coasting Hill Pavilion
Southern façade. View of the meadow

252
The Coasting Hill Pavilion. The Round Hall

253
The Coasting Hill Pavilion. The Round Hall
Vase: *An Allegory of Water*. 19th century
The Meissen Porcelain Factory
After a model by JOHANN KÄNDLER
Porcelain

254 >>
The Coasting Hill Pavilion
The upper platform of the vestibule
Grille. 1769. By I. FURSTICK, after
a drawing by ANTONIO RINALDI. Chased iron
Sculpture: *Apollo and Daphne*. 19th century
Sculptor: RAFFAELLO ROMANELLI, from the
original by GIANLORENZO BERNINI. Marble

255
The Coasting Hill Pavilion
The Porcelain Study. Porcelain group

256
The Coasting Hill Pavilion
The Porcelain Study. Porcelain group:
Neptune and Thetis. 1774. The Meissen
Porcelain Factory. After a model
by JOHANN KÄNDLER

257
The Coasting Hill Pavilion
The Porcelain Study. Porcelain group
over the fireplace

258
The Coasting Hill Pavilion
The Porcelain Study

259
The Coasting Hill Pavilion
The Porcelain Study. Porcelain group:
Apollo. 1772–75. The Meissen Porcelain
Factory. By Johann Kändler
and Michel Victor Acier

260
Pond near the Chinese Palace
Sculpture: *Jonah*. By an unknown
18th-century sculptor, from the original
by LORENZO LOTTO. Marble

261
The Chinese Palace. View of the
southern façade from the pond
Architects: Antonio Rinaldi, 1762–68;
Andrei Stakenschneider,
Ludwig Bohnstedt, 1852–53

262
The Chinese Palace
Detail of the southern façade

263
The Chinese Palace. The Blue Drawing-Room

264
The Chinese Palace. The Damask Bedchamber
Ceiling painting: *Urania Training a Youth*
1760s. Painter: DOMENICO MAGIOTTO

265 >>
The Chinese Palace
The Damask Bedchamber

266
The Chinese Palace
The Pink Drawing-Room

267
The Chinese Palace. The Hall of the Muses

268
The Chinese Palace. The Hall of the Muses

269
The Chinese Palace. The Hall of the Muses
Painted decoration of the eastern wall
*Terpsichore, the Muse of Choral Song
and Dancing.* 1768. Painter: STEFANO TORELLI

270
The Chinese Palace. The Buglework Cabinet

271
The Chinese Palace. The Buglework Cabinet
Detail of a buglework panel

272
The Chinese Palace. The Great Hall

273
The Chinese Palace. The Great Hall
Low-relief: *Peter the Great*
Sculptor: Marie Anne Collot. 1769. Marble
Medallion. Early 1770s. By Giacomo Martini,
Kozma Kotelnikov and Fiodor Biriukov
Red and blue smalts, gilt copper and enamels

274
The Chinese Palace
The Lilac Drawing-Room
(The Stucco Room)

275
DOMENICO CIGNIAROLLI
Angelica and Medoro. 1760s
Oil on canvas

276
The Chinese Palace
The Small Chinese Cabinet

277
The Chinese Palace. The Small Chinese
Cabinet. Vase and two *famille-verte* figures
17th century. China. Porcelain

281 <<
The Upper Park
Sculpture: *The Three Graces*
Early 19th century. By an unknown sculptor,
from the original by Germain Pilon
Bronze

282
The Peter Bridge across the River Karost

283
The Upper Park. *Laocöon*. 1817
Sculptor: Ch. Crosatier
From the ancient original. Bronze

GATCHINA

The creation of one of the best known and most distinctive palaces in Russia was recorded in an inscription on a brass plate: "Founded on 30 May 1766, completed in 1781." The plate was still in place in the 1950s on the elegant portico that adorns the central section of the Gatchina Palace on its park façade.

The Gatchina palace was constructed for Count Grigory Orlov. He was presented with the manor of Gatchina in 1765 in gratitude for his part in the palace coup of 20 June 1762 that brought Catherine the Great to the Russian throne. Such a generous reward came as no surprise to contemporaries: Grigory Orlov was not simply Catherine's lover, but also one of the chief figures in the Russian state at the start of her reign, the Empress's closest and most trusted advisor.

The palace was built to the design of the Italian architect Antonio Rinaldi (1709–1794). He came to St Petersburg in 1754 and became architect to the heir to the throne, Grand Duke Piotr Fiodorovich (the future Peter III) and his wife, the future Catherine the Great. Orlov's choice of Rinaldi was evidently influenced by the Empress who appreciated the architect's tremendous skill and refined taste.

The clear understated architectural forms employed by Rinaldi in the palace accorded with the tendencies that marked the period of transition between the Baroque and the Rococo. The Italian created "a country house in the new taste" that called for "refined simplicity" and a close relationship between the building and its natural setting. The twentieth-century architect Nikolai Lanceray stated: "In this building Rinaldi set himself the task of reproducing the 'real' Classical Renaissance, without any accretions, almost without decorations." The harmonious unity of palace and park was achieved by constructing open arcades on the ground floor of the central block that were linked together by a passageway running through the building. The material used to face the palace – local Pudost limestone that required neither plastering nor painting – further enhanced the impression of a natural link between it and the surrounding landscape. Compositionally, the building consisted of a combination of different volumes that set each other off. Besides, placed as it was on the on the highest point of a hill above the south shore of the White Lake, the edifice dominated the entire surrounding area.

Work on the park began at the same time as the construction of the palace – in the late 1760s. Grigory Orlov was a passionate huntsman and intended to use the manor as a hunting estate. Consequently work on the Gatchina park began with the establishment of a large game-reserve – the Menagerie. It was crossed by a number of broad, straight cuts that divid-

ed the woods up into squares. At the meeting points of these cuts, large areas were cleared, providing a good view in all directions. Within the enclosure of the Menagerie deer, wild goats, hares and other animals lived wild until they were rounded up by drivers during hunts.

The services of a leading expert in park design, the Englishman Joseph Bush, were enlisted for creation of the Gatchina park. At that time a shift was taking place away from the regular parks of the first half of the eighteenth century, with their geometrical lines and areas decorated by statues and fountains, and towards landscape parks that imitated virgin nature. The creators of such parks sought to produce the illusion of a stretch of countryside untouched by human hand. Bush was succeeded by James Hecket. He entered service with Count Orlov and worked at Gatchina for more than sixty years, dying here in 1833 at the age of 96. In his will, he wrote: "It pleased fate to so arrange matters that I, a foreigner, found myself a new kindly homeland – Russia and permanent residence in Gatchina..." One of the provisions of Hecket's will was the establishment of a fund "for the assistance of the poor and orphans, primarily those to be found in Gatchina." Hecket's fund operated right up to 1917.

The beauty and originality of Gatchina were brilliantly brought out by its master gardeners. The keynote Black, White and Silver Lakes are located at the centre of the park ensemble and form the dominant compositional element. The natural outlines of the White Lake, its headlands and shallow bays were adorned with great taste by the planting of stands of trees and shrub-

Unknown artist. *Portrait of Count Grigory Orlov*. 1770s (?). Oil on canvas

View of the Gatchina Palace from the Vauxhall. 1880s. The Imperial Porcelain Factory, St Petersburg. Porcelain plaque

Portrait of Antonio Rinaldi. 1782 Bas-relief. Sculptor: FEDOT SHUBIN Marble

reminded contemporaries of Prussia, a state whose practices and procedures the Grand Duke considered exemplary at that time. Prussian military regulations were also taken as a basis when the famous "Gatchina forces" were being created. The impressions Paul brought back from his journey around Western Europe in 1781 and 1782, especially those of Chantilly in France, the residence of Princes de Condé, were reflected in the subsequent development of the ensemble. Work only really got under way here in 1792, as the Grand Duke, occupied with the construction of Pavlovsk and the organization of his "Gatchina army", had very limited funds. Construction in the palace was carried out to the designs and under the supervision of Vincenzo Brenna (1747–1818), a native of Florence. The architect had been working in Russia, for the Grand Duke's "lesser court", since 1784. Beginning as a humble assistant to Charles Cameron, Brenna gradually became the leading architect of the court, Paul I's favourite builder.

In 1792–93 the small wooden Pavilion of Venus was erected on the artificial Island of Love. Surrounded by water on three sides, the pavilion seems to grow out of the White Lake. Between 1792 and 1795 the Large Terrace Landing-Stage appeared on the shore of the same lake – one of the finest and most striking architectural features of the Gatchina park.

Not far from the Island of Love in the years 1794–96 a finely proportioned Classical portal was constructed, designed as a sort of propylaeum by the architect Vincenzo Brenna.

beries. The relatively small Silver Lake is remarkable for the depth, clarity and emerald tint of its water. Originally the park was not rich in architectural structures, in full accordance with the character of early landscape parks in the eighteenth century. Three small works have come down to us from that period: the Chesme Obelisk, the Octagonal Well and the Eagle Column.

In 1783 Grigory Orlov, the owner of Gatchina died, and Empress Catherine purchased the estate from his heirs. On 6 August that same year, she granted it to her son Grand Duke Paul who was master here for almost eighteen years. The Tsesarevich was delighted with this gift and wrote to Metropolitan Platon: "The place is in itself most pleasant, and the sign of favour in itself dear." Paul turned the Gatchina estate into a little realm that

Not by chance this original piece of architectural scenery came to be known as the Mask Portal: it was intended to mask from view the pavilion called the Birch House that looked like a stack of firewood from the outside but was exquisitely decorated inside.

In 1794–95, on an artificially raised area of land beneath the palace windows, the Private Garden was laid out containing works by Italian sculptors, trellises and straight alleys converging on a central round area. Alongside the Lower Dutch Garden was constructed in imitation of the type of garden common in Holland, where the chief decorative element is brightly coloured flower beds. The Lower Dutch Garden is adjoined by the Upper Dutch Garden, set on terraces linked by striking flights of stone steps. The terraces of the Upper Garden descend to the Carp Pond, an artificial basin in the shape of a jug.

The 1790s saw the appearance of the rest of the architectural features in the Gatchina park: the Farm, the Eagle Pavilion, the Connetable Obelisk, the Forest Orangery, the Amphitheatre and the Admiralty. Entrances of different design were set up on the boundaries of the park – the Admiralty, Birch, Sylvia and Menagerie Gates. The extensive bodies of water that occupy a quarter of the park led to the appearance of a large number of bridges. In the 1790s seven of the original wooden bridges were replaced by stone ones that are among the most perfect-looking structures in the whole Gatchina ensemble.

In the spring of 1796 building work began in the palace under Brenna's direction. The architect turned the open loggias of the semicircular arms into enclosed galleries in which he created new state rooms – the Crimson Gallery (later the Gallery of Arms) and the Greek Gallery. The closing in of the loggias was a consequence of Rinaldi's engineering miscalculation (the columns had by this time begun to break under the excessive load placed on them) and also of the unsuitability of this architectural form for the northern climate. At the same time the arcades of the main block were closed in and an original looking Vestibule appeared in place of the open passageway.

Five days after he succeeded to the throne, on 11 November 1796, Paul I granted Gatchina a town charter. The Emperor intended Gatchina to become an exemplary town for the Russian Empire. The palace was redesigned in keeping with its new status as an imperial residence. The single-storey square blocks at the ends of the galleries were extended upwards to two and a half storeys. Rooms for members of the imperial family and also a palace theatre were created in one of them, known as the Arsenal Block. The other, Kitchen Block, housed the palace church that went back to Orlov's time, service rooms and premises for the courtiers. The green meadow in front of the palace gave way to a parade ground enclosed by a moat crossed by wooden drawbridges.

The changes to the façades of the palace led to a reworking of its interior decoration. The state rooms on the main floor of the central clock were given an emphatic grandeur. This was also the location of the personal apartments of Paul I: the Emperor spent a considerable part of his time in the Oval and Tower Studies.

The very end of the eighteenth century was marked by the contributions to the Gatchina palace and park ensemble of two Russian architects: Adrian Zakharov and Nikolai Lvov. Late in 1799 on Paul's orders Zakharov was appointed architect of the town of Gatchina "while remaining in his post with the academy" at a salary of three thousand roubles a year. He completed work on the reconstruction of the Kitchen Block and reconstructed the palace church within it to his own design. In the park the same architect created such brilliant features as the Aviary, the Three-Arch (Lion) Bridge on the Great Porkhov Road and the Hump-backed Bridge. Sadly, the construction of a number of Zakharov's projects was halted following the death of Paul I. The most significant of those projects was a monastery on the edge of the park – a rare example of this architect employing the devices of mediaeval building. Had the work been completed, the monastery would undoubtedly have become one of the gems of

ings, including *The Banishment from Paradise* by the Italian artist Luca Giordano and *Storm* by the celebrated French seascape painter Joseph Vernet, were introduced into the Anteroom.

Kuzmin's concept called for a restoration of the visual dominance of the central block that had been lost when the side blocks were raised to the level of the galleries and accordingly a further tier was added to each of the pentagonal towers. The bastion wall in front of the palace was also altered: the grille was replaced by a continuous parapet of local limestone with embrasures and bastions for cannon, while the wooden bridges were replaced by four stone ones.

A notable event in the history of the Gatchina Palace took place on 1 August 1851 – the unveiling of the monument to Emperor Paul I. The model for the sculpture was produced by the famous sculptor Ivan Vitali on the basis of the well known formal portrait of the Emperor by Stepan Shchukin that had been approved by Paul himself. During the parade of guards that was held to mark the unveiling, eight-year-old Grand Duke Nikolai Alexandrovich (the eldest son of the future Alexander II), dressed in the uniform of the Life Guards Pavlovsk Regiment, marched at the head of the first platoon of that regiment. His six-year-old brother, Alexander Alexandrovich (the future Alexander III), dressed as a private of the regiment, with a tall pointed shako on his head and a rifle at his side, stood guard by the monument. Did that small boy standing by the statue of his great-grandfather understand the significance of the event? Perhaps on that very occasion the interest in Russian history that contemporaries noted in Alexander III was born.

After the reconstructions of the mid-nineteenth century no more substantial alterations were made to the appearance of the palace. Subsequent owners limited themselves to redecorating the apartments they occupied to their own taste. The work done in the 1850s enhanced the castle-like character that the palace had acquired in the late eighteenth century.

Between 1881 and 1894 the Gatchina Palace was the residence of Emperor Alexander III who spent a considerable part of the year here. Again, as at the end of the eighteenth century, the palace was at the centre of public life in the country. A succession of technological innovations were introduced into the life of the court: electric lighting, running water, drains, the telephone. Throughout the nineteenth century the work performed in the park was mainly aimed at preserving the appearance that it had acquired in the late eighteenth century.

After the February Revolution in 1917 the fate of the former imperial residences, including Gatchina, became an issue. In late

the Gatchina ensemble. The Priory Palace, erected on the shore of the Black Lake in 1797–99 to Lvov's design, has an unusual appearance. It is noteworthy both for its architecture and for the unique beaten earth method used in its construction.

After Paul I's death in 1801, Gatchina passed to his widow Maria Fiodorovna. The Dowager Empress devoted most of her efforts to charitable activities and so no major work was carried out in the palace. Only in 1809–11 were some changes made to the interiors of the main block under the direction of Andrei Voronikhin in order to make the palace suitable for habitation in the winter months.

In 1828, after Maria Fiodorovna's death, Gatchina passed to her son, Emperor Nicholas I. In 1844–56 the last major reconstruction of the palace was carried out under the direction of the architect Roman Kuzmin (1811–1867). Kuzmin had a masterly command of different architectural "idioms" and finished the State Vestibule, Marble Staircase and Rotunda beneath the Coat of Arms in the spirit of the Renaissance, the Chinese and Gothic Galleries with elements of mediaeval Gothic architecture, and a number of living rooms in the Rococo style. The two square blocks were dismantled and re-erected using the old foundations and part of the old walls. As before, apartments for the imperial family were installed in the Arsenal Block, but effectively the architect turned it into a new palace with over two hundred rooms that housed unique collections of art works: Chinese porcelain, bronzes and portraits. In the central block the State Staircase was decorated with views of Gatchina and Pavlovsk painted by Semion Shchedrin and his pupil Andrei Martynov and this led to some changes to the interior. Paint-

May a commission began working to receive and make an inventory of the museum property. The commission included the prominent art historians Count Valentin Zubov (who later became the first director of the Gatchina Palace Museum), Piotr Veiner and Alexander Polovtsov. On 19 May 1918 the Gatchina Palace, opened its doors to visitors. The former imperial residences became institutions of an entirely new type – state-owned palace museums. In the words of Balayev and Pomarnatsky, experts in the field, "the special value of the palace museums lay in their documentary authenticity, convincingly reflecting whole periods in history and the artistic culture of the past. The Gatchina pal-ace museum was in this respect of thoroughly exceptional value as its walls contained historical–artistic and domestic complexes of rooms spanning, when taken together, a large historical space of time – from the mid-eighteenth century to the eve of the October Revolution."

Before the Second World War, the Gatchina Palace was one of the largest of the palace museums in the environs of the former capital and deserved its fame as "the suburban Hermitage". Its displays and stocks numbered over 54,000 items.

Following the Nazi invasion, S. N. Balayeva, the chief curator of the palace, and I. K. Yanchenko, a researcher, organized the evacuation of the most precious pieces (more than 8,000 items were sent to the rear of the country, another 3,000 were moved into Leningrad, to St Isaac's Cathedral). In 1944 work began on the restoration of the park and palace after the devastating fire that took place in January that year. In 1950 restoration work was suspended. After a long break, in the spring of 1976 the restorers returned to the palace. The first recreated rooms in the palace were opened on 8 May 1985. As of today eight historical interiors on the main floor of the central block have been restored.

The state rooms begin with the Anteroom that has been restored to its appearance at the end of the eighteenth century, disregarding the alterations made in the middle of the nineteenth century. The parquet floor, intarsia doors and door architraves of pinkish orange artificial marble belong to Rinaldi's

The Marble Dining-Room, one of the most striking rooms in the palace, was created by Brenna in place of two rooms of the old, Orlov, palace. The main decorative element is sixteen columns of Italian marble. The hall has two ceiling paintings. One, *Hope and Love*, is the work of an unknown eighteenth-century artist; the other was produced by the restoration artist B. L. Golovanov on the basis of a copy of the painting *Selene and Endymion* by the eighteenth-century Venetian artist Stefano Torelli.

The Upper Throne Room of Emperor Paul I was embellished in the late eighteenth century by three Gobelins tapestries. Two of them – *Asia* and *Africa* – are from the *Countries of the World* series, the third, *Ceres*, from the *Gods and Goddesses* series was placed above the fireplace on the wall opposite the windows. In 1797 a carved and gilded wooden throne upholstered in crimson velvet was installed here.

The pride of the Throne Room is a magnificent parquet floor made from precious varieties of wood to the design of Antonio Rinaldi. The enfilade of state rooms is continued by the Crimson Drawing-Room with an interior that echoes that of the Throne Room. Three Gobelins tapestries from the celebrated *Don Quixote* series formed a continuous covering on the walls of the room.

The State Bedchamber, decorated by Brenna, includes the ceiling painting *The Marriage of Psyche* by Doyen that was installed here in 1799. *The Marriage of Psyche* was the best ceiling painting in the palace and was recreated in the studio of Ya. A. Kazakov.

The Throne Room of Empress Maria Fiodorovna adjoins the White Hall. It was originally known as the Picture Room as it housed a collection of Western European painting. The decoration did not change in character even after 1797 when a throne and dais for the Empress was placed here and the ceiling painting *Apollo and the Muses* installed.

The third storey of the central block at present houses an exhibition of items from the museum's stocks, featuring painted portraits of the eighteenth and nineteenth centuries and works of decorative and applied art.

The Gatchina Palace is not only a monument of Russian artistic culture, but also a monument of the nation's history. The chronicle of events is reflect in it, as if in a drop of water, from the palace coup of 1762 right down to developments in present-day cultural and political life. It has known the brilliant heights and the depths of forty years of post-war oblivion. But the fruitful labours of restorers and staff of the Gatchina Palace make it possible to state with assurance that the worst in its long and difficult history is behind it. The amazing story of one of Russia's most outstanding architectural masterpieces goes on.

original decoration of the room. Brenna added a ceiling painting, decorating the remainder of the ceiling and the coving with moulded representations of ancient helmets, shields, banners and single-headed eagles. At the present time the Anteroom contains *Faith and Love*, a work by an unknown eighteenth-century artist.

The maid decorative element of the Passage Room is an oval marble bas-relief – a portrait of Antonio Rinaldi by the Russian sculptor Fedot Shubin that was installed here in the late eighteenth century. The ceiling of the Passage Room takes the form of an elliptical dome. Similar domed ceilings existed originally in other rooms of the main floor, but were later hidden by ceiling paintings. Here the dome has survived and gives the room a special charm.

The White Hall is the largest of the state rooms. Here, to a considerable extent. Rinaldi's decoration has been preserved: the magnificent parquet of different woods, the exquisite stucco work on the walls and ceiling, the doors, reddish artificial marble architraves and sculptural compositions above the doors. Brenna installed bas-reliefs, some of them genuine ancient works, in the walls. The sculptural and moulded decoration was complemented by marble busts, statues and vases. The hall contains the ceiling painting *An Allegory of the Birth of a Hero* by Gabriel François Doyen, a pupil of Carle Van Loo.

284 <
View of the Gatchina Palace from the
parade ground. Architects: Antonio Rinaldi,
1766–81; Vincenzo Brenna, 1796–1800;
Roman Kuzmin, 1845–56

285
The Gatchina Palace. The White Hall
Architects: Antonio Rinaldi, 1770s;
Vincenzo Brenna, between 1797 and 1800

286
The Gatchina Palace. The Anteroom
Architects: Antonio Rinaldi, 1770s;
Vincenzo Brenna, between 1797 and 1800

287 >>
The Gatchina Palace. The Marble Dining-
Room. Architect: Vincenzo Brenna,
between 1797 and 1800

288
The Gatchina Palace
The Upper Throne Room of Emperor Paul I
Architects: Antonio Rinaldi, 1770s;
Vincenzo Brenna, between 1797 and 1800

289
The Gatchina Palace
The Upper Throne Room of Emperor Paul I
Tapestry: *Ceres* from the series *Gods*. 1770s
After a cartoon by Claude Audran

290 >>
The Gatchina Palace
The Upper Throne Room of Emperor Paul I
The throne of Emperor Paul I. 1797
By Christian Meyer. Replica of the throne
of Empress Anna Ioannovna
(1731, by Nicholas Clausen)

291
The Gatchina Palace. The Crimson
Drawing-Room. Architect: Vincenzo Brenna,
between 1797–1800

292
The State Bedchamber. 1872
Watercolour by Luigi Premazzi

293 >>
The Gatchina Palace. The Throne Room
of Empress Maria Fiodorovna
Architect: Vincenzo Brenna,
between 1797 and 1800

294
The Gatchina Palace. Exhibition "Paintings
and Objects of Decorative and Applied Arts
from the Collections of the Gatchina Palace"
The Room of Children's Portraits

295
The Gatchina Palace. Exhibition "Paintings
and Objects of Decorative and Applied Arts
from the Collections of the Gatchina Palace".
The room with the portrait *Emperor
Paul I in Maltese Garments*
by SALVATORE TONCI

296
ANTON LOSENKO
Portrait of Grand Duke Pavel Petrovich as a Child. 1763. Oil on canvas

297
GEORG CHRISTOPH GROOTH
Portrait of Empress Elizabeth Petrovna
About 1744. Oil on canvas

298 <
VLADIMIR BOROVIKOVSKY
Portrait of Empress Maria Fiodorovna. 1796
Sketch. Oil on canvas

299
The Gatchina Palace. Items from
the Hunting Service. 18th–19th centuries
The Imperial Porcelain Factory, St Petersburg;
the Meissen Porcelain Factory

300
The Gatchina Palace. Decorative plate
depicting the double-headed eagle. 1840s
The Imperial Porcelain Factory, St Petersburg

301
The Gatchina Palace. Dish showing a view
of the Gatchina Palace from Long Island
1820s. The Imperial Porcelain Factory,
St Petersburg

302
The Gatchina Palace. Cup and saucer
featuring Emperor Alexander II encircled
by officers. 1870s. The Imperial Porcelain
Factory, St Petersburg

303
The Gatchina Palace. Vase. 1860s–1870s
The Imperial Porcelain Factory,
St Petersburg

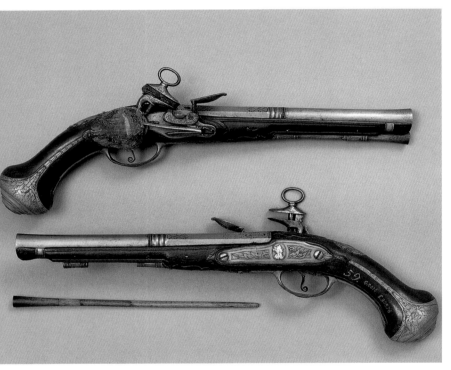

304
The Gatchina Palace. Flintlock rifle
1747–49. By J.-H. Stockmar,
Suhl, Germany

305
The Gatchina Palace. Pair of wheel pistols
1750s. Rinoi (Catalonia), Spain

306
The Gatchina Palace
Flintlock five-barrelled rifle. 1730s
By J.-A. Hermann, Wiesenthal, Germany

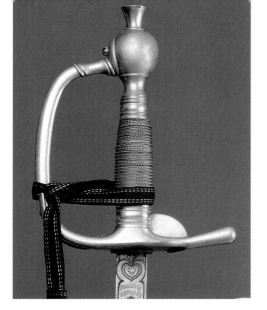

307
The Gatchina Palace. Cavalry officer's
sword, model of 1798. Hilt. 1890–1900
By Schaff, St Petersburg

308
The Gatchina Palace. Powder-box
18th – first half of the 19th century
Russia

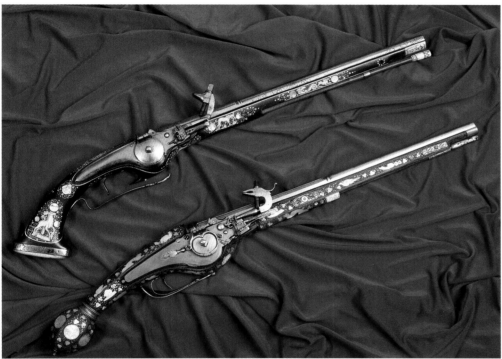

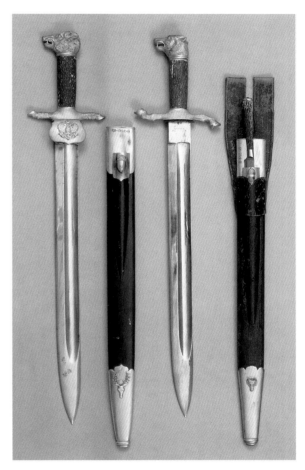

309
The Gatchina Palace. Pair of wheel pistols
1640–50. Silesia

310
The Gatchina Palace. Daggers of court
hunting officers, model of 1855. 1870s
The Schaff Factory, St Petersburg

311
The Gatchina Palace. Pair of wheel pistols
1580. Dresden, Germany

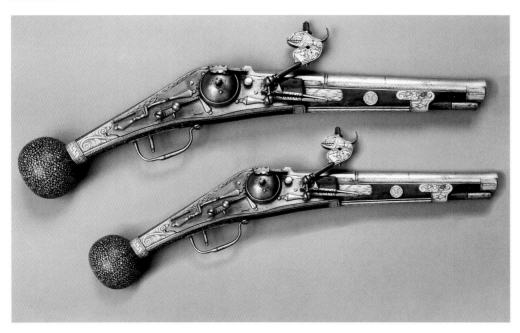

312
The Gatchina Palace
The underground passage
Architect: ANTONIO RINALDI

313
The Gatchina Park
View of the Gatchina Palace
from the Carp Bridge

314
The Gatchina Park. View of the Large
Terrace and the Gatchina Palace from
the White Lake. The Large Terrace
Architect: Vincenzo Brenna, 1792–95

315
The Gatchina Palace. The Vestibule
Architects: Antonio Rinaldi, 1770s;
Vincenzo Brenna, between 1797 and 1800

316
The Gatchina Park near
the Carp Pond

317
The Gatchina Park
View of the Gatchina Palace
from the Carp Pond

318
The Gatchina Park. The Private
Garden. 1794–95. Sculpture
18th century. Italy

319 <<
The Gatchina Palace. The park façade

320
The Gatchina Park. The Birch House
Architect: HENRI FRANÇOIS GABRIEL
VIOLLIER (?), 1780s. The Mask Portal
Architect: VINCENZO BRENNA, 1794–96

321
The Gatchina Park
The Venus Pavilion on the Island of Love
Architect: VINCENZO BRENNA (modelled on
a pavilion at Chantilly), 1792–93

322 <<
The Gatchina Park. The Chesme Obelisk
Architect: Antonio Rinaldi, mid-1770s

323
The Gatchina Park. The Carp Pond
Architect: Vincenzo Brenna (?),
late 18th century

324
The Gatchina Park. The Priory Palace
Architect: Nikolai Lvov, 1797–99

325
The Gatchina Park
Interior of the Birch House

326
The Gatchina Park. The Birch House
Ceiling painting: *Zephyr with a Garland
of Flowers*. Late 18th century. By an unknown
painter. Recreated in the 1970s by
the artists O. Pedayas, B. Golovanov
and R. Slepushkina

327 >>
The Gatchina Park. View of the Birch
House and the Mask Portal

Императорские резиденции
окрестностей Санкт-Петербурга.

Петергоф, Царское Село, Павловск, Ораниенбаум, Гатчина

Альбом (на английском языке)

Издательство «Альфа-Колор», Санкт-Петербург
Тел./Факс (812) 326-8384 E-mail: alfac@mail.wplus.net

Printed and bound in Finland